The Complete Book of

CHILD
SAFETY

The Complete Book of

CHILD
SAFETY

Dr Douglas Cohen, Dr Henry Kilham,
Professor Kim Oates

impact books

This edition first published in Great Britain 1993 by
Impact Books, 112 Bolingbroke Grove, London SW11 1DA

First published in Australia 1989 by
Simon and Schuster Australia
20 Barcoo Street, East Roseville NSW 2069

ISBN 1-874687-17-X

Cover illustration by Martin Salisbury
Illustrations bu Martin Salisbury and Troy Newton (pages 53 and 72)
Typeset by Concept, Crayford
Printed and bound by The Guernsey Press, Guernsey

Contents

Foreword

There can be no doubt about the importance of accidents in the field of child health today. As HRH The Princess of Wales, who is Patron of the Child Accident Prevention Trust, has said, 'Tragically, accidents are still the commonest cause of death among toddlers and young children. And all too often these accidents could have been prevented with careful attention from adults – not only parents, but designers, planners and manufacturers. I believe it makes sense to commit resources to prevention rather than pay for the consequences.'

This book aims to give practical down-to-earth advice on child safety and accident prevention. Not only does it give advice about making your house and garden safer and about road safety, but it looks too at the safety of toys, playground equipment and many other aspects of child safety. Advice is given on the different dangers that are relevant to different age groups, and it deals with the topical problems of 'stranger-danger' and physical and sexual abuse.

It has been written by three Australian practitioners with many years of experience, both as parents and as members of the staff of the Children's Hospital in Sydney.

Douglas Cohen was Head of Surgery until his retirement in 1985. He was founder and Director of the Child Safety Centre in Sydney, and was the first Chairman of the NSW Branch of the Child Accident Prevention Foundation in Australia. He was awarded the Order of Australia in 1981 for services to paediatrics. He is now living in London, where he is Honorary Consultant to the Child Accident Prevention Trust.

Professor Kim Oates set up the Child Development Unit at the Children's Hospital. He was Director of Medical Services until 1985, when he was appointed Professor of Paediatrics and Child Health at the University of Sydney. He has written extensively about child health.

Dr Henry Kilham was Head of the Intensive Care Unit at the Children's Hospital for many years. He is Physician in Charge of the NSW Poisons Information Centre, and is also an authority on child drowning.

The original Australian version of this book has already been very successful in that country, and it is with great pleasure that the Child Accident Prevention Trust has collaborated in producing an English version. The Child Accident Prevention Foundation of Australia and the Child Accident Prevention Trust in this country were founded about the same time, and both aim to reduce the incidence and severity of injury to children.

We believe that this book will help to protect children at home, at play and at large in the world.

Dr Hugh Jackson, OBE, MC, FRCP
Child Accident Prevention Trust

Preface

Children are a great source of joy to their parents – but they can also be a source of anxiety!

It is a fact, however, that no matter how alert we are, our curious, active children, in the normal course of *being* children, can get into scrapes and, even more worrying, they can have accidents which can injure them in ways that a band-aid and a kiss can't fix.

But with planning and forethought it is quite possible to work out the potential danger zones and take care of them before the worst happens. It just takes common sense and an attitude of 'when in doubt, keep it out of reach'. Careful planning and the use of safety catches on cupboards, child restraints in cars, child-resistant caps on medicine bottles and so on, will go a long way to making a safer environment for our children.

We should try to make home as safe a place as possible, but thought must also be given to the protection of our children outside their homes. Proper attention to road safety, play safety and protection from the dangers they may meet in our busy world are also important. Although being a parent to a bundle of energy can seem daunting, it really isn't too difficult!

With many years of experience both as parents and paediatricians in a large children's hospital, we have seen the effects of a wide range of accidents. We have come to know how accidents can happen, and we have learnt how, with a sensible approach, they can be avoided.

You will find a lot of practical information in *The Complete Book of Child Safety*. We look at ways to make your house safer and provide advice about safety in the garden. We look at features in children's toys which may prove dangerous, and suggest which toys are best for different ages, as well as giving advice about such things as playground equipment and pets. Other chapters include road safety, information about safety for your children when travelling to and from school, babysitters and safety during holidays.

There are special sections about the different dangers that are particularly relevant to different age groups, 'stranger danger', non-accidental injuries and finally a section on basic first aid procedures in case of emergency.

Our aim is to help you protect your children at home, at play and at large in the world.

Douglas Cohen
Henry Kilham
Kim Oates

Chapter

1

DIFFERENT DANGERS AT DIFFERENT AGES

Types of accidents depend on the child's age. A nine-month-old baby does not break bones from skateboard riding, but can be injured by rolling off a change table. In thinking about accident-prevention it is helpful to be aware of the main dangers to children at different ages. It may also help to think about the four important principles which relate child development to child safety.

▶ *Never underestimate the rapid rate of a baby's development* Most books refer to the average baby, but anyone who has children knows that all babies are different. Some children develop skills faster than others. This means that just because it was safe to leave potentially dangerous things lying around the house yesterday, because they were 'out of reach', it may not be safe today: your child may now have learned to crawl, and be able to get into all sorts of danger.

▶ *Always be prepared for the unexpected* Children constantly surprise us with the dangerous situations into which they can get themselves. Part of a parent's job is to anticipate such potential dangers. There is no substitute for careful supervision particulary with young children.

▶ *Children think differently from adults* Although they learn from experience, very young children cannot always generalize from one situation to another. This means that even though a toddler is injured falling from a climbing frame, he or she may not be able to understand that there can be a similar danger at the top of a staircase. Younger children tend to have 'magical thinking'. This

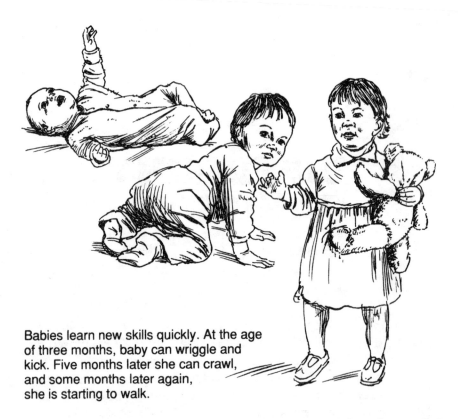

Babies learn new skills quickly. At the age
of three months, baby can wriggle and
kick. Five months later she can crawl,
and some months later again,
she is starting to walk.

means that they think they have far more power than they really
have. They may believe that they can stop a speeding car, or
bounce it away from themselves. This can clearly lead to dangerous situations.

▶ *Children cannot always see the consequences of their actions* This
makes it difficult for them to realize that if they get into a
dangerous situation, such as jumping into a swimming pool before
they can swim, they could sink to the bottom and not be able to
get out again.

All of this means that children, especially young children, have to be
carefully supervised. It also means that the key dangers will vary
according to the child's age. This chapter highlights some of these
key dangers.

Birth to six months

Babies usually cannot roll over until they are four to five months old.
Up until this age accidents generally occur because of something the

parents do to the child, such as giving the wrong medicine, or giving too much medicine or letting the baby slip out of their hands. Babies at this age need close supervision and gentle care. As the baby gets closer to six months and begins to be truly mobile, the accident rate increases.

The bath

Always check the water temperature first. Use your elbow, as it is a sensitive spot. Do not let the baby go while it is in the bath and never, leave it alone in the bath, even for a few seconds. If you must attend to something urgently, take the baby with you.

Falls

Once the baby starts to roll, at about four to five months, he or she can roll off the changing mat or fall from a table or bed. The cot is a safe place when the sides are up. A playpen on the floor is also a good spot. Try not to leave the baby alone on a table or bed, even for a moment. Bouncing cradles are fun for babies, but keep them away from areas where family members usually walk. Tripping over a baby in a bouncer is not good for the baby or for the person who trips. *Never*

put baby bouncers on tables or work surfaces. The baby is likely to bounce right off the edge. Baby bouncers bounce, but babies do not.

Pushchairs, cots and carrycots

Remember that a parked pushchair, like a parked car, should always have the brakes on. You do not want your baby to roll away. Make sure that your pushchair cannot fold up suddenly. It should have a safety locking device to prevent this from happening. Adopt the habit of always using a harness for the pushchair.

Make sure your baby's cot and mattress conform to safety standards. The recommended distance between cot bars is 2.5–6.5 centimetres to avoid heads becoming trapped. Is there a gap between the mattress and the cot side? Can your baby breathe if his or her face is against the mattress? It is better not to use a pillow for babies under one year old.

Never have any strings or ribbons in the cot that can become entangled around the neck. Does the side of the cot lock securely into position when raised? Never leave your baby alone in the cot without raising the cot sides. Carrycots have a tendency to tip. Tying the handles together will help to make the carrycot more stable.

Sunburn

A baby's skin is very delicate. Even periods as short as twenty minutes on a very hot day can cause nasty burns. Use sun hats, suntan lotion and avoid long periods in the sun.

Car transport

Do not cuddle your baby in the car. Babies should only travel in cars if they are in an approved safety restraint. In car accidents, enormous forces occur, and it is just not possible for a parent nursing a baby to protect it. Makeshift car restraints are useless; only use restraints made by reputable manufacturers. Crashing into a stationary object at a speed as low as 40 kilometres per hour causes the same force as a child falling two storeys onto concrete. The only way to have protection, as well as by driving safely, is to use an approved child safety restraint.

Of course, a young child must never be left alone in a parked car, even if you think it will only be for a few moments.

Toys

Toys should be too large to swallow, too tough to break and have no sharp points or edges. Unbreakable rounded toys of smooth wood or firm plastic are safe. Cuddly toys are good, but make sure they are well made and that the eyes do not come loose.

Sharp and small objects

Keep pins and other sharp objects out of baby's reach. Buttons, beads and other small objects should also be kept out of the way.

Clothing

Avoid elastic which is too tight and cords and ribbons which become loose and wind tightly around toes and fingers or even the neck. Anorak hoods for young children should not fasten with cords.

Medicines

Doses have to be accurate. Always read instructions carefully, and measure out doses with a dropper or syringe. Make sure the medicine you are giving is one which has been prescribed for the baby, and only give medicines on medical advice. Make certain that your chemist dispenses all tablets in child-resistant containers or in strip or blister packs. The Pharmaceutical Society now insists on this as a 'professional requirement' unless the recipient requests otherwise.

Pets

Pets and children are a combination which brings joy. But babies cannot get away or defend themselves at all. Keep pets away from young babies unless you are there to supervise. They will have time to enjoy them when they are older.

Six to twelve months

This is a time when great strides in development are made. Children in this age range learn to sit, to crawl and to stand. They learn to pull themselves up on all sorts of things, and may pull some of them down on top of themselves. Between six and twelve months new and interesting objects are all put into the mouth. It is a time of great fun for a parent, and a time when the baby becomes a mobile, young explorer. It is also a time when parents have to watch extra carefully, and make sure that their home is safe.

The kitchen

Beware of things which hang down. The tablecloth might seem just the thing for a baby to grab hold of to get into the standing position. The baby is not to know that there may be a cup of hot coffee on it

which he or she will spill. Replace tablecloths with placemats at this age. Make sure that electric cords do not dangle down to tempt your baby. Check the cupboard under the sink. It is just the sort of place the baby will want to explore, to touch and taste everything in it. Store oven cleaners and detergents in a safe, secure place, well out of baby's reach. Knives, scissors and any sharp or pointed utensils should be out of reach and out of sight in a closed drawer.

Other rooms

Put small, sharp objects well out of reach. You may have to reorganize your house for a while, but it is worth it. Put a baby gate at the top and bottom of staircases. Lamps and sharp-edged furniture can be hazardous. Electric power points have a fascination for this age group; use safety covers. In the bathroom, take special precautions against scalds, drowning, poisoning, scissors, razors and cosmetics.

NOTE. ⚠ indicates that the situation illustrated is dangerous.

Burns

Burns happen quickly. Some clothes catch fire when very close to a fire without actually touching it. Try to buy clothing labelled as flame-resistant. Put guards in front of heaters and open fires. Never leave your baby alone near heaters, open fires, or barbecues.

Poisons

Many tablets look like sweets. Do not keep unwanted or unfinished medicines 'just in case'; get rid of them by flushing them down the toilet. Do not keep medicines in your handbag; babies love to explore the contents of handbags. This means that you will have to remind visitors – especially grandmothers who may be taking some sort of tablet – to keep handbags out of your baby's reach. Make sure that those medicines and tablets which you do keep are prescribed in child-resistant containers and kept in a child-resistant cupboard.

Never store detergents or oven cleaners in a kitchen or laundry cupboard under the sink – your baby will soon find them.

Dummies

The most serious accidents with dummies occur from choking on a broken piece of the dummy or from swallowing or inhaling an unfastened dummy pin. Many parents find a dummy helps to pacify their baby, but if your baby is happy without a dummy so much the better. Do not fasten the dummy to clothes.

High chairs

Make sure your high chair has a wide, stable base so your baby cannot tip it over. The chair should have a harness fitted to prevent your baby trying to stand up. Always check that it is fastened. Make sure the tray locks into position, to prevent fingers becoming trapped or pinched. Try not to leave your baby unattended in the high chair. Never put your baby in a chair or baby bouncer on the table. Your baby might easily fall off. 'Table chairs' are not recommended.

Baby walkers and pushchairs

Baby walkers are not recommended. They are hard to steer and hard to stop. They allow a baby to move about at a time when he or she has no awareness of dangers such as stairs or fires, and they also help the baby to reach and grasp things previously inaccessible. There is no evidence that baby walkers help babies to walk any earlier.

In pushchairs, the restraining straps should be firmly adjusted. When waiting to cross the road, do not let the front of the pushchair protrude over the gutter – cars sometimes come too close.

Playpens

Make sure that the bars of the playpen are 7.5–10 centimetres apart and that the sides are at least 60 centimetres high. Wooden playpens are preferable to those with mesh sides. Remember that your baby can use large toys placed in the playpen to climb over the top and fall out.

Toys

Toys should be safe and interesting. Small, detachable parts are dangerous at this age, as everything is tested by popping it into the mouth. Toys do not have to be expensive: children at this age like

cardboard boxes, wooden blocks and simple things. Mechanical and battery-operated toys impress the parents more than the baby.

One to two years

Your child is now more mobile, able to walk confidently, and is interested in climbing. He or she has not yet learned that what goes up must come down. He or she will open drawers and doors, take things apart and enjoy playing with water. Children at this age have a poor sense of danger, and so need the combination of being in a safe environment and being under close supervision. The main danger at this age is still lack of supervision. As well as wanting to explore, children approaching two years want to be independent. They want to try to do things themselves. This desire to be independent, coupled with as yet imperfectly developed co-ordination, an inability to perceive danger and to understand the consequences of actions, as well as difficulties in controlling impulses, explains why toddlers have the highest rate of accidents.

Play areas

A large part of the child's time may be spent in the kitchen. It is an interesting area, but one with potential dangers. Keep pot handles turned away from the edge of the stove, and keep electric cords from such things as kettles, toasters and irons out of reach. Remember the danger of cleaning agents kept under the kitchen sink. You removed them for the baby under one year – keep them removed. If you are working in the kitchen, put baby in a playpen where he can see and hear you.

Your child will be interested in exploring outside areas, so keep outside doors securely fastened to prevent him from wandering off. Outside play areas should be well fenced.

Water

This age group is fascinated by water. Never leave the child alone in the bath or around open areas of water. Even small garden ornamental ponds and other shallow water is dangerous. Swimming pools are a special hazard. Children should never be left alone, even for 'just a few seconds' near a swimming pool.

Poisons and other harmful things which are swallowed

Keep tablets locked up. Do not leave then in a handy place, such as by the bedside or on the dresser or table. This could also be a handy place for your exploring toddler. Throw out old tablets and medicines, and keep the ones you need out of reach and out of sight in a child-resistant cupboard. (Remember that nothing can be made truly childproof yet still be usable by adults. We asked a four-year-old boy to open a strong plastic medicine container with a pound coin inside and a child-resistant cap in place. After trying unsuccessfully to remove the cap, he broke the container with a hammer!)

Peanuts are a particular hazard at this age. They can easily slip down the wrong way and lodge in the upper airways or lungs. If you are entertaining friends do not leave peanuts on the coffee table where your toddler can get them – a good rule for peanuts is keep them away from children under four. Although peanuts are the most common cause of choking episodes in young children, any small object is a potential cause (for example, a bead, button, or the small part of a toy.) Alcohol is also a danger for the inquisitive toddler; do not leave unfinished glasses around. The curious toddler might finish them off, and it does not take much alcohol seriously to harm a small child.

Peanuts, buttons and beads

Rebecca's family doctor was concerned enough to refer her immediately to the Children's Hospital, which is where I met her, and her parents, Katie and John.

During the night Rebecca had developed a wheeze and cough, and the following morning she seemed sufficiently unwell for Katie to take her to their doctor. After listening to her lungs, and not much liking what he heard, he sent her to us.

After examining Rebecca I sent her to X-ray which showed a partial collapse of the right lung. As a result, Rebecca was given an anaesthetic that afternoon, and a fine tube was passed down her throat and into her lung airways. The cause of the problem was soon discovered – a peanut was wedged in the main airway to the right lung. Skilfully the surgeon eased the peanut out and withdrew it with a pair of fine forceps.

John and Katie were amazed that a peanut could have found its way into Rebecca's lung. 'But I thought that she'd coughed it up!' exclaimed Katie. At my questioning look she explained that they had had friends in for drinks the night before. Rebecca had been allowed to stay up to say hello to them, and her parents had only discovered that she had been helping herself to some nuts when she started to cough and splutter. 'I thought that one must have gone down the wrong way, but she seemed to recover quickly and I took her straight up to bed.'

After a night in hospital Rebecca was none the worse for wear and Katie and John were able to take her home. But they never left peanuts within reach again.

If you have young children make sure that any small objects such as buttons, beads, coins, and particularly peanuts, are kept well away from them. Pen tops and button batteries are also especially dangerous. Children will put all kinds of things into their mouths and small items can easily cause them to choke.

Outside the house

The garage is a fascinating place but make sure that sharp tools are put away and that petrol, paint cleaners and pesticides are stored securely. Always store paraffin and paint cleaners in their original containers, with child-resistant caps, never in cups or soft-drink bottles.

When coming in and out of your drive by car, remember that toddlers are hard to see. Drive slowly, look carefully and always check behind the car before reversing.

Three to four years

The three-year-old now has many skills. He or she climbs and runs, plays with other children, may ride a tricycle, may cross the street and may be out of sight for increasingly long periods. There always seems to be a hurry to get things done. Patience is not a common virtue at this age. The world is seen only from the child's point of view. In fact he or she may still think the world was created entirely for his or her benefit.

There is difficulty in understanding cause and effect relationships and children at this age think that just because they do not want something to happen (such as falling from the top of the tree they have just climbed), it will not happen. This is 'magical thinking', but it does not protect children from falling out of trees. It may even lead them into dangerous situations. They also have trouble understanding that things they see on television may not be real and they may try to imitate some of these events. Children at this age still need supervision but are starting to learn safe behaviour. It is a good time to be teaching them about safety.

Outside the house

Make sure that dangerous and poisonous objects in the garage are locked away. Now is the time to give even more emphasis to teaching about road safety. Teach children how to cross roads and make sure they only cross with an adult. Warn them of the dangers of running out from between parked cars to chase a ball which has gone into the road. Make sure that outdoor play areas are safe.

Burns

Fire and matches will be starting to have a fascination. Do not leave matches and cigarette lighters around. Teach children about the danger of open flames. Wearing a full skirt near a fire is dangerous – serious and sometimes fatal burns can occur. Avoid long, flimsy nightwear near fires or electric radiators: tracksuit-type pyjamas are much safer.

Glass doors and windows

The impetuous youngster is likely to run straight through a glass door or panel. Make sure glass panels and doors are clearly marked with an adhesive strip at a child's eye level. All glass in doors should be safety glazing (BS 6206, Class C). Alternatively, cover the glass with plastic safety glazing film.

Shower screens are safer if they are made of safety glass. Be careful with glass-topped coffee tables. Your youngster may decide to sit in the centre of it and crash right through. Glass-topped tables should be made with safety glass that meets the British Standard (BS 6206 Class C). It is not a good idea to let your child walk around while drinking from a glass or carry glass bottles.

Swimming pools

The hazard of drowning at this age is still high. Even if your child has had swimming lessons, your responsibility to supervise constantly near the pool is not reduced. It is one thing for a child to be able to swim across a pool in a controlled situation into the waiting arms of a parent or swimming instructor, it is quite another thing for a child to fall into a pool and panic. Having taught your child to swim does not in any way reduce your responsibility to provide constant supervision when your child is at the pool.

If there is a home pool, it should be fully enclosed by a safety fence with a self-closing gate which meets the British Standard.

Five to eight years

Your child is now at school and away from home for a large part of the day. The risk of bicycle and traffic injury increases, and parent example about safe road behaviour is essential. School-age children want social acceptance, so that gaining approval from their friends might be more important to them than conforming with their parents' wishes. Sometimes to gain the approval of other children there is daring and adventurous behaviour. The younger children in this age group still do not fully understand cause and effect, so that they might attempt certain activities without detailed planning and without considering all the possibilities. What the child might conceive as being a daring escapade can lead to a serious accident. Children at this age also start to become interested in rules. This is helpful for parents, as they can involve their child in formulating safety rules. Children are more likely to adhere to rules which they have had a hand in making.

Road safety

Pedestrian safety applies particularly to children under eight years. The rate of death in this age group is over twice that seen in older children and adults, with the exception of the very old.

Teach your child about pedestrian crossings, and about how to cross the road at traffic lights. Most importantly, teach by example. It is important to teach children that, because they are not very tall, drivers might find them hard to see. Tell them too that although pedestrian crossings are recommended, they should not assume that cars will always stop. Teach them to wait until the approaching car slows down before they step on to the road at the pedestrian crossing.

If your child walks to school alone, plan a walking route to school with as few road crossings as possible.

Fire

Fire still holds a fascination at this age. Make sure that children know the dangers of flammable liquids such as methylated spirits and paraffin. These must be kept well away from fires, incinerators and barbecues.

Have smoke alarms fitted in your home, making sure that they are properly sited.

Electricity

The age has passed when objects are poked into power points, but children now want to start using electrical appliances themselves. Teach by example, so that they know that they should always turn off power points before removing plugs.

It is desirable to have an earth-leakage circuit breaker fitted to protect all electrical outlets. All electrical wiring should be checked and installed by a licensed electrician.

Swimming

Your child should start to learn to swim from the age of about five. Swimming lessons are more effective at this age. Even though some younger children can be taught to swim, they are most receptive to swimming instruction, and can be taught in a short time, from about five years of age. Supervision around pools is still essential, and children must never be left alone near the swimming pool.

Nine years and over

This is an age where there is much more independence. Supervision becomes less important, as by this time the child should have been taught safe behaviour. Children now have more responsibility for their own safety, although there is still the temptation to engage in risk-taking behaviour with encouragement from their friends.

Bicycles

Safety helmets should be worn, and your child should learn the road rules. Even at this age bicycles should not be ridden on busy roads.

Skateboards

Skateboards are fun, but your child should be encouraged to wear protective clothing and must avoid roads.

Tools, domestic appliances and other sharp objects

Children should be taught to use domestic appliances and tools properly. Teach them, when using a knife, to cut away from themselves, and when they are helping around the house, show them the proper care and maintenance of equipment.

Summary

It is helpful to think about the risks facing your child in terms of his or her particular stage of development. Children face different dangers at different ages. Remember:

▶ children develop faster than you expect
▶ you must always be prepared for the unexpected
▶ children do not think the way adults do
▶ children may not be able to predict the consequences of their actions

Chapter

2 THE SCOPE OF THE PROBLEM

Causes of accidental death

Every year in England and Wales, as a result of accidental injury:
- ▶ 700 children die
- ▶ 120,000 require admission to hospital
- ▶ 10,000 children are permanently disabled

Two-thirds of all childhood deaths occur in the first year of life, and almost half of these take place in the first month. Complications arising from premature birth, congenital defects and cot death (sudden infant death syndrome) are the major causes of death in an infant's first year. Only one in forty deaths of children under twelve months results from accidental injury.

The number of deaths resulting from accidents rises during the toddler years (one to four years). In this age group the two major causes of death are accidents and congenital defects. The two most common fatal accidents are those occurring in and around the home and traffic accidents. In the home, burns and scalds head the list of fatal accidents, followed by suffocation and drowning. Almost one in every twenty deaths in this age group is due to accidental injury.

Toddlers have their accidents mainly in the home. School-age children have fewer accidents in the home but more at school, in sport and at play. They are especially at risk of road accidents as pedestrians and when riding bicycles. Children aged ten to fourteen years are nearly twice as likely to be taken to hospital as a result of an accident as a toddler.

The number of deaths occurring in England and Wales among children in different age groups is shown in Table 1 which also illustrates the fact that boys are at greater risk of serious injury than girls. This pattern is not confined to Great Britain. In all countries where accident statistics are available it has been shown that boys are almost twice as likely to have an accident as girls.

Fatal accidents
(by age and sex)

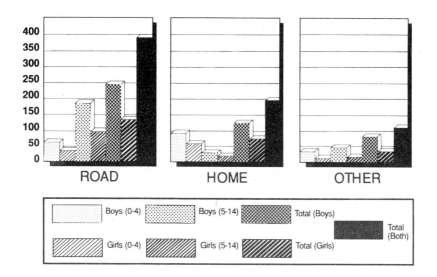

Table 1

Fatal accidents (by age and sex)

	0–4 years		5–14 years		totals		
	boys	girls	boys	girls	boys	girls	both
road	61	37	184	99	245	136	381
home	95	57	28	17	123	74	197
other	32	15	46	17	78	32	110

Figures are from the Office of Population Censuses and Surveys and are for England and Wales for 1987

Children from economically deprived social groups have been shown to run a greater risk of suffering serious injury. This particularly applies to burns and scalds. There are a number of factors that contribute to this:

▶ less satisfactory housing in terms of location of space
▶ lack of money to maintain potentially dangerous equipment
▶ inadequate property maintenance
▶ lack of money to buy safety equipment such as fireguards
▶ poor play facilities – playing on the streets
▶ overcrowding increases the risk of injury – especially fire

Changes in the pattern of childhood accidents over the years

Since the beginning of the century there has been a progressive decline in the number of children dying from all causes. This has been particularly marked in infectious diseases since the introduction of antibiotics in the 1940s. We have seen a dramatic decrease in the number of deaths among children, not only from infectious diseases but also from congenital deformities, leukaemia and malignant disease. Most life-threatening epidemic diseases have been virtually eliminated from developed countries. After the newborn period, death from accidents is at least twice as common among children as any naturally occurring disease. In developed countries accidents to children must be regarded as the major public health problem of the twentieth century.

The death rate from accidents has declined but not so dramatically as in the case of disease. This is in large part due to improvement in intensive care and operative techniques. Until the mid-1970s statistics showed a progressive increase in the number of children admitted to hospital with accidents, but since then there has been a steady decline. There has been a marked decrease in fatal road traffic accidents to children since 1970. Child pedestrian fatalities have been halved but fatal accidents to child cyclists and children in cars have not been reduced significantly.

There was a steady increase in home accidents until around 1975, after which there has been a slow but continuing fall. There has been a marked fall in the number of deaths from drowning – from around two hundred per year up to 1974 down to about fifty in 1987, in spite of an increase in water sports.

Where do accidents occur?

Road accidents

These represent only about 2 per cent of all children's accidents but cause about 55 per cent of all accidental deaths. Injuries resulting from road accidents tend to be more extensive and disabling than those caused by other accidents. Furthermore, certain types of accidents, particularly those related to bicycles, tend to be under-reported. It is likely that as many as 70,000 children are injured each year while riding bicycles but only 7,500 of these are reported to the police.

Home accidents

Home should represent safety and security. Yet three-quarters of a million children are injured in the home every year. Many home accidents could be prevented by the use of simple and inexpensive safety equipment, such as child-resistant caps on medicines, and by parental supervision and example. This particularly applies to the more serious home injuries – burns and scalds, poisoning, injuries from broken glass and falls from one level to another.

Accidents outside the home

Table 2 shows that almost 1.2 million children in England and Wales are injured outside the home each year. It is not surprising that there are differences between toddlers and school-age children which reflect where they spend most of their time and the greater lack of danger-awareness in the younger children.

Table 2

Accidents outside the home

	0–4 yrs	5–14 yrs
Recreational areas	**22%**	**17%**
playground	10%	5%
parks/countryside	6%	8%
other areas	6%	4%
Sporting	**5%**	**18%**
indoor	1%	4%
outdoor	1%	12%
swimming pool	3%	2%
Public Buildings	**11%**	**4%**
Educational areas	**15%**	**27%**
creche/nursery	8%	-
school	2%	11%
school grounds	5%	16%
Street	**39%**	**27%**
Other locations	**8%**	**7%**
Annual National Estimate	**186,000**	**1,004,000**

Figures from Dept Trade & Industry Leisure Accident Surveillance System (LASS)

Why do children have accidents?

There has been a progressive reduction in the incidence of industrial and motor vehicle accidents but, although there has been some improvement in the prevention of home accidents, they continue to occur in substantial numbers, predominantly affecting the young and the very old. Over 50 per cent of all accidents to our children happen in and around the home. Why do these accidents continue to happen?

Accidents outside the home

0 - 4 YEARS

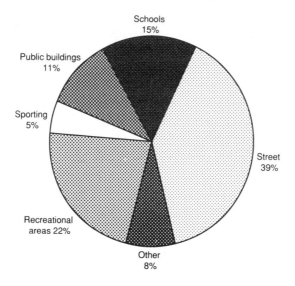

Accidents outside the home

5 - 14 YEARS

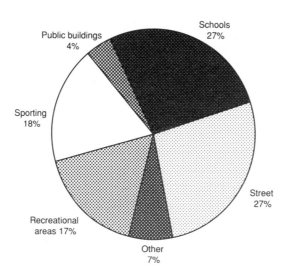

There are a number of reasons. Firstly, there is the sheer magnitude and diversity of childhood accidents. Secondly, adequate funding must be provided to deal with the problem. Thirdly, we must dispel the dogma of inevitability which is based on a number of assumptions, mostly incorrect.

Accidents only happen to *other people's children.*	All children are prone to suffer accidents – including your own.
Accidents are largely determined by stress and anxiety existing between parents and children.	Stress is only one factor in causing accidents.
In this technological age accidents must happen and will continue to happen with increasing frequency.	Not so – there has been a steady decline is child injuries for many years.
Risk-taking is an integral part of human nature.	True.
All children must inevitably suffer some accidents – it is part of the learning process.	Child safety is *injury* prevention rather than accident prevention.

Although there are certainly a number of factors in accident causation, their existence does not absolve us from the responsibility of making our environment safer, of anticipating and preventing certain accident situations and from providing adequate supervision and safety education for our growing children.

The children who are most at risk of accidents in the home are those aged between one and five years. So in planning an accident prevention programme, special attention must be given to this high-risk group.

As illustrated in Figure 1, there are four important parameters to consider. From birth onwards there is a progressive learning process which includes the ability to assess risk-taking. This learning process can be reinforced and accelerated to some extent by judicious example

Figure 1

Four parameters of the learning process

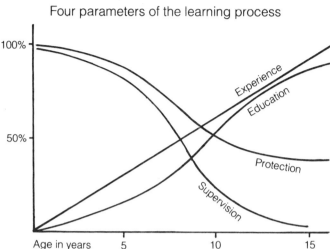

and education, but in the early stages a high level of supervision and protection must be provided. Experience and education permit the progressive withdrawal of such supervision and protection. Certain minor accidents, which will inevitably occur, may justifiably be regarded as part of this learning process.

What we are aiming at is not necessarily to prevent *accidents* but to prevent *injury*.

Does the accident-prone child exist?

By adult standards all young children are accident-prone:
▶ they lack experience
▶ they lack foresight
▶ they are physically and emotionally immature

But are there some children who are more vulnerable to injury than their peers, and can we identify them? I would suggest to you that there are. Some children are born vulnerable, some achieve vulnerability and some have vulnerability thrust upon them.

Reference has already been made to the progressive increase in the degree of responsibility which a child is able to take as he grows older. In order to do this a child needs to be able to comprehend dangerous situations and needs the mental ability to transfer knowledge gained from experience to new and somewhat different situations.

Therefore the child with an intellectual handicap or a sensory-apparatus defect – such as impaired sight or hearing – will be handicapped in learning where danger lies. Language and reading disabilities are also important, while children suffering from other developmental handicaps which contribute to the syndrome of *minimal brain dysfunction* – clumsiness, attention span deficit, lack of concentration, emotional instability, left/right confusion and abnormal impulsiveness – will also be disadvantaged.

Physical handicaps also present an added risk if a child is slow in his movements or lacks co-ordination. Additional problems may be created if children are over-protected and are not allowed progressively to fend for themselves. Danger comes not only from inexperience generated by over-protection but also because such children rebel against what they see as unnecessary restrictions, and indulge in risk-taking. These are the children who are born vulnerable.

There is an association between stressful events in the home and accidents. Emotional stresses directly affecting the child or between the parents are reflected in the child's behaviour. They are shown by such features as regression to more infantile behaviour – bed-wetting or thumb-sucking – deterioration in performance or, at times, self-injury. Disobedience and risk-taking can be manoeuvres to seek attention which may lead to injury. These are the children who achieve vulnerability.

It should also be remembered that child abuse frequently presents as an 'accident'. It is estimated that at least 10 per cent of child injuries seen in hospital are due to child abuse and a further 10 per cent are associated with gross neglect. In the case of older children, it is estimated that only about half of the suicide attempts are recognized as such. The remainder are listed as 'accidents'.

Children who have vulnerability thrust upon them are the product of the socially disadvantaged and multi-problem families. Housing and play facilities may be inadequate, parent figures are often absent, or they lack any consistent training or example. Every community has its proportion of unreachables and unteachables.

In such instances, attempts at safety education are doomed to failure. These unfortunate children may develop precocious survival techniques appropriate to the urban jungle in which they live, but this does not compensate for the dangers which surround them.

The philosophy of injury prevention

The aim of this book is to increase awareness of the dangers facing our children and to highlight ways in which these dangers can be minimized. The philosophy is one of *injury* prevention. It is based on the important principle that, by and large, *accidental injuries to children are not inevitable.* The possibility of most major accidents can be foreseen, and with intelligent planning can be avoided. Many 'accidents' in the home are trivial, and can be regarded as part of the learning process. Our concern is with those accidents which cause *injury.*

Education in child safety, aimed at producing greater community awareness, is the key to accident prevention. Experience has shown, however, that there is little value in short safety campaigns. Education needs to be ongoing, and it needs to be directed at parents and children, at teachers, at legislators and at all concerned with the design of products and of the environment.

Also of importance in any accident prevention programme is the development of safety standards and the collection of home and leisure safety data on a uniform national basis. The extent of the problem needs to be identified and areas which require special attention need to be pinpointed. In addition, the effects of any safety measures need to be carefully evaluated. This can only be achieved with the support of the Government.

There are a number of organizations which are addressing this important problem. The Child Accident Prevention Trust is a scientific advisory body concerned with all aspects of accidents in childhood. It became an independent charitable Trust in 1981. The Trust concentrates on establishing the causes and patterns of child-hood accidents, their resulting injuries, and methods of reducing their number and severity. It is gratifying that the Trust has seen fit to associate itself with *The Complete Book of Child Safety.*

The Consumer Safety Unit of the Department of Trade and Industry has, since 1976, collected systematic information about home accidents through the Home Accidents Surveillance System (HASS). This is done by collecting information from twenty hospitals in England and Wales.

By 1987 the Council of the European Communities had intro-duced the European Home and Leisure Accident Surveillance System (EHLASS). HASS has accordingly been expanded to include leisure accidents and to include information from Scotland and Northern Ireland.

The development and review of safety standards is also important in any accident prevention programme. This is the responsibility of the British Standards Institute. When it is deemed that a particular standard should be mandatory rather than voluntary, the necessary regulations and legislation are matters for the appropriate government department.

Finally, mention must be made of the Royal Society for the Prevention of Accidents (RoSPA). This important body deals with accidents in both adults and children. It has divisions which deal with occupational safety, road safety, home safety, agricultural safety, water safety and safety education.

A comprehensive list of organizations concerned with child safety appears at the end of this book.

Summary

Considerable progress has been made in the area of child safety in recent years but much remains to be done.

We have reviewed causes of accidental death in childhood and emphasized the increasing importance of accidents as a cause of child death. We have examined what causes child accidents and whether some children are 'accident-prone'. Finally we have put forward our philosophy of child safety.

Child accident prevention remains a major health problem in Great Britain, as in all developed countries. It is only through increased awareness of the dangers which continue to face our children and by the refinement and maintenance of appropriate safety standards that some of the many injuries and deaths suffered by the nation's children can be prevented.

NOTE. The statistical information in this chapter is derived from *Basic Principles of Child Accident Prevention,* prepared by Dr Michael Hayes and Dr Gordon Avery and edited by Andrew Benson for the Child Accident Prevention Trust, 28 Portland Place, London, W1N 4DE. Copies of this monograph are available on application to the Trust.

The section 'Does the accident-prone child exist?' is based on a paper presented by Dr Helen Connell at a symposium on Child Accident Prevention held in Brisbane, Australia in 1979. It was subsequently published by the Child Accident Prevention Foundation of Australia as Chapter 22 of *Accidents to Children* edited by John Pearn.

Chapter

SAFETY INSIDE THE HOME

More than half of all accidents to young children occur in and around the home. Although many of these are minor, a significant number of children are killed or seriously injured each year in home accidents.

A look at the figures for Great Britain, compiled by the Child Accident Prevention Trust (CAPT), gives us an insight into the main danger areas inside the home, the articles within the home most commonly associated with accidents, the type of accidents that occur and the nature of the injury.

Of the 250,000 children admitted to hospital each year in Great Britain following an accident, 22 per cent occur in circulation spaces – that is, the entrance hall, stairs and landings – and over half of these result from falls, mostly on stairways. Almost 18 per cent occur in the kitchen, the majority of these being burns or scalds, and 4 per cent occur in the bathroom, most commonly due to either scalds from hot water or to falls in and around the bath. Approximately 36 per cent of home accidents occur in living and dining areas, and 15 per cent of these occur in the bedroom. Less than 20 per cent of home accidents occur outdoors.

The Home Accident Surveillance System (HASS) in their most recent report (1989) looks at home accidents sustained by children under five years old, the most vulnerable group. Home accidents to children tend to be age-related, with a peak incidence around the age of two. This relates to their ability to crawl, walk and climb into danger, and to their natural tendency to put things into their mouths.

Access to the hazards that exist in every home needs to be

restricted by mechanisms that will keep very young children separated from the hazard, or will at least slow them down or deter them until an adult intervenes. A good example is the use of child-resistant caps on potentially dangerous products such as sleeping pills or sink-cleaners.

However, it must be remembered that all accidents do not lead to injury. Many minor accidents can be regarded as part of the learning process. Children can be taught that stoves are hot, that knives are sharp and that matches can burn, without necessarily getting hurt.

Children under nine months of age have limited mobility, but they can wriggle, kick or roll into hazardous situations. They also start to sit, crawl and reach out for objects which they often put into their mouth.

HASS data shows that more than half the accidents in this age group are due to falls – off furniture or work surfaces, from bouncing cradles, or out of cots or prams. As they start to move around they can fall down stairs – baby walkers are particularly dangerous in this respect. Over half the injuries involve the head or the face.

Between nine months and five years children become more mobile. They learn to stand, walk and run. They start to climb and to go up and down stairs. Because of their mobility and curiosity they are more likely to suffer burns and scalds, poisoning, cuts, or to ingest or inhale foreign bodies.

The most common and the more serious types of home accidents to young children are:

▶ falls from one level to another, particularly onto hard surfaces; most commonly off or into furniture or down stairs
▶ cuts from knives and sharp utensils, household appliances and toys
▶ scalds related to the kitchen, the bathroom and to cups or containers of hot liquid in living areas
▶ burns from fires or contact with hot surfaces
▶ swallowing or inhaling foreign bodies, particularly peanuts
▶ poisoning by medicinal products, such as sleeping or heart pills, and other substances stored in the kitchen, like oven and sink cleaner or bleach
▶ drowning in the bath
▶ electrocution due to faulty wiring, power points or appliances

Consideration will now be given to ways of reducing these potential hazards. These recommendations can be incorporated in new houses, or when renovations are being carried out, without adding significantly to the cost. When additional cost is involved this

will frequently be offset by reduced maintenance. Nor have we taken into account the value of children's lives and limbs.

> NOTE. Statistics quoted are based on information from the Home Accident Surveillance System (HASS), 1987. They include all accidents for which treatment was sought at an Accident and Emergency Department.

Circulation spaces

Circulation spaces include the entrance hall, stairs and landings
Number of accidents each year – around 55,000
Commonest cause – over half of them are due to falls on stairways

Because falls make up a large proportion of home accidents, the safest houses are those on one level. A two- or three-storey house may well be unavoidable, but remember that they are significantly less safe and that extra safety measures will need to be taken.

Split level or single steps are best avoided when possible. If such a design is already present, the step should be clearly defined.

▶ Stairways should be designed in a U or L shape when possible, with a landing halfway down. This means that there is not so far to fall, and consequently there will be fewer injuries.

▶ Avoid winding or tapered stairs. Risers should be of a uniform height. In general, the construction of stairways should conform to British Standard 5395.

▶ Banisters should be provided. These should be designed so as not to provide a foothold for climbers. The gaps between the vertical rails should be less than 100 millimetres so that a child's head cannot squeeze through. Banisters on landings need to be higher than those on the stairs.

▶ The hand rail should be designed to ensure that movement of the hand along the rail is not hindered.

▶ Fixed carpeting should be fitted to minimize the impact of falls. Stairways should not be constructed with open risers.

▶ Halls, stairways and landings should be provided with adequate lighting.

▶ Doors or windows should not encroach onto stairs or landings.

▶ Never site glass windows or doors at the foot of stairs. If they are already present, install safety glass.

Steps and stairs are inherently unsafe. Falls on steps or stairs account for 10–13 per cent of injuries requiring medical care. The most effective means of preventing falls on stairways is a stair gate at the top and bottom of the stairs, which is properly fitted according to the manufacturer's instructions, and is used regularly.

The kitchen

Number of accidents every year – 44,000
Commonest accidents – scalds from hot water
                     – burns from cookers
                     – ingestion of cleaning products

Ideally, a kitchen should have only one entrance so that it is not used as a thoroughfare. This permits a child-resistant barrier to be installed at the entrance.

Where a single entrance is not feasible, the general layout of the kitchen should ensure that traffic through the kitchen does not impinge on the *work triangle* consisting of the sink, refrigerator and cooker. Some suitable layouts are shown in Figure 2.

A clear space of at least 1.2 metres should be allowed in front of all kitchen fittings. This distance provides an adequate work space that is not too cramped. Where benches are installed opposite each other, a clear space of at least 1.5 metres should be left between them.

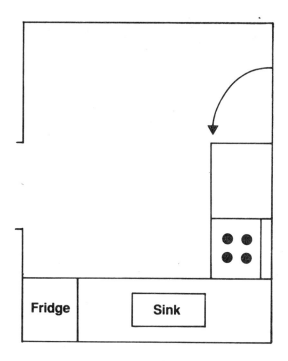

**Figure 2
L-Shaped Kitchen**
No likelihood of collision but children cannot be excluded from the work areas.

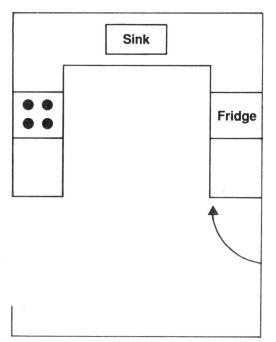

U-Shaped Kitchen
Safest because they are cul-de-sacs and can be fenced off but still allow supervision.

Consider putting your baby in a playpen in the kitchen, or where he can see you, while you are cooking.

Stoves and appliances

▶ Do not position kitchen cupboards over the cooker.
▶ Doors should not impinge on the work space in front of the oven or cooker.
▶ Do not install the cooker in an island unit. These are very accessible to children.
▶ The cooker should have a work surface at least 300 millimetres wide on each side. A separate oven needs a work surface of the same width adjacent to it.
▶ Work surfaces should be on the same level as the cooker in order to allow saucepans and pots to be slid across with minimal risk.
▶ Do not site the cooker in front of a window. The wind may blow curtains across the cooker, and they may catch fire. If you have a gas cooker, one of the jets may blow out. If a fire starts on the cooker, an escape route from the kitchen may be blocked.
▶ Controls for the cooker should preferably be on top and not at the front of the unit, so that they are out of reach of young children.
▶ Upright stoves should be firmly fixed to the wall, and floor ovens should preferably be hinged vertically in order to prevent children standing on the oven door. A wall oven is safer still.
▶ Power points should be installed away from both the sink and the hob to avoid the risk of cords trailing across the burners.
▶ Use either coiled flexes or cords that are as short as possible so that they do not hang down over the end of the bench.

Cupboards and floors

▶ Provide at least one child-resistant cupboard in the kitchen, and one in the utility room, if this is separate.
▶ Keep detergents and household cleaning products out of reach, *never* below the sink. If you have young children, keep these things in a cupboard fitted with a child-resistant catch.
▶ If medicines are stored in the kitchen the same rules apply.
▶ Out of reach means at least 1.75 metres above the floor, where a child under six years cannot reach or climb.
▶ Never store household cleaning products or medicines in the same cupboard as food items.
▶ Cupboard doors should slide or open fully to lie flat against adjacent cupboards.
▶ Rounded edges on bench tops are preferable to square edges.

▶ Ensure that all floors in the kitchen and laundry areas have a slip-resistant surface.

Bathrooms and toilets

Number of accidents each year – 10,000
Commonest accidents   – scalds from hot bath water
                       – falls in the bath or shower
                       – drowning in the bath while unsupervised
                       – cuts (razors or broken glass)
                       – poisoning from medicines or cosmetics
                       – electrocution

The bathroom door

The door to the bathroom should have a latch fitted at least 1.5 metres above the floor to prevent unsupervised entry by young children. The latch should be able to be opened from both sides of the door, to prevent anybody from being trapped in the bathroom. If privacy locks are fitted they should likewise be designed so they can be opened from either side of the door. When planning a new house or undertaking major renovations, plan to have a toilet in a separate room, if possible, so that access to the bathroom can be restricted without denying access to the toilet.

Hot water and heating

Turn the thermostat on your hot water system down to 54 degrees Celsius, but remember that water even at this temperature needs only thirty seconds immersion to produce a scald. Fit safety taps or thermostatically controlled mixer valves to all hot water outlets, and ensure that all hot water pipes are insulated or concealed to prevent burns.

Electric radiators in bathrooms should be mounted on the wall not less than 2 metres above the floor. All light and power switches in the bathroom should be fitted with pull cords.

If heated towel rails are fitted, make sure that they have thermostatic controls to reduce the chance of burning. The thermostat should be set at 54 degrees Celsius.

All power and light outlets should be permanently wired by a licensed electrician. An earth-leakage circuit breaker should be installed to protect the whole house against any danger of electrocution.

The bath and shower

The bath and shower should have slip-resistant surfaces and the bath should have a safety grip handle. Soap holders should be recessed. Shower screens should be made from toughened plastic or safety glass complying to British Standard 6206 (Class C). Never allow a toddler to run his or her own bath water. Always turn on the cold water before adding the hot. Be wary of bath heaters supplying instant hot water. They tend to produce boiling or near-boiling water which can produce a severe burn. Always supervise young children when in the bath or shower. Try to avoid leaving them alone in the bathroom, even for a few seconds.

Fixtures, fittings and floors

- A cupboard with a child-resistant catch should be provided for the storage of medicines, razors and other potentially hazardous items.
- Remember that cosmetics can be poisonous, so keep them out of the reach of young children.
- Make sure that the washbasin, toilet or cupboards do not provide a climbing route to the bathroom window.
- Ensure that the washbasin does not overhang the end of the bath.
- Floor-mounted or pedestal washbasins are to be preferred. Avoid wall-mounted washbasins unless secure fixing with bolts can be ensured.
- The bathroom floor should be carpeted or have a slip-resistant finish.

Household fittings

Annual accidents in living and dining areas – 90,000
Annual accidents in bedrooms – 38,000
Most common accidents are   – falls
                              – burns or scalds
                              – poisoning

When building a new house or renovating an old one, care needs to be taken when choosing household fittings as many are potentially hazardous to children, particularly to young children.

Doors

Annual accidents involving doors – 36,000

Fit all external doors with a latch not less than 1.5 metres above the floor to prevent young children leaving the house without supervision. Doors should, whenever possible, open against a wall so that they do not encroach into the space where a child is playing. Where space is limited, consideration should be given to the use of sliding or folding doors. Internal doors should have handles low enough to enable young children to open them readily except for the bathroom, kitchen and laundry doors.

Avoid glass panels in doors, particularly at the foot of stairs or at the end of a passage where a child might slip and fall into them. All glass in doors should be safety glazing conforming to British Standard 6206 (Class C). Glass doors should be clearly marked at eye level for both adults and children.

Sliding doors which open on to a balcony, yard or garden should be locked or have their travel restricted so that a young child cannot open them more than 10 centimetres.

Windows

Annual accidents involving windows – 6,500
Annual falls from windows – 1,500

Windowsills above the ground floor should not be easily climbed or provide a ledge for sitting on.

Care should be taken in the design of windows to ensure that they can readily be used as an emergency exit in the event of fire, while at the same time having restricted access for young children.

All windows with openings less than 1.2 metres above the floor should be designed or modified so that a young child cannot open them more than 10 centimetres. Horizontally-hinged windows are particularly dangerous.

All windows coming to within 80 centimetres of the floor should be fitted with safety glass complying with British Standard 6206 (Class C).

Consider using high level bolts on upstairs windows to prevent them being opening by children.

Remember that with young children there is the risk of strangulation whenever a cord long enough to encircle the neck is within reach. This includes cords for blinds and curtains.

Electrical installations

All electrical installations should be done by a licensed electrician.

Sufficient power points should be provided to minimize the use of double adapters or extension cords. At least the following number of power points is recommended:

bedroom	3	kitchen	6
dining room	2	laundry	3
living room	4	garage	2
bathroom: shaver point only			

▶ Install light switches at both the top and bottom of stairs wired so that either switch can control the light.
▶ Mount power points in the kitchen at least 1.5 metres above floor level and out of the reach of young children.
▶ All power points within the reach of young children should have either safety shutters or safety plugs.
▶ Install residual current circuit breakers for additional protection against electrocution.
▶ Make sure all fuses are wired correctly.

Heating

Annual accidents from heating equipment – 14,500

Many types of heating are dangerous to young children. An open fire is very pleasant but is particularly hazardous. Young children should never be left in a room with an open fire without supervision. If you have an open fire, slow combustion heater or free-standing stove, enclose it with a nursery style fireguard that conforms to British Standards. Gas and electric fires should be fitted with fireguards that conform to BS 1945.

The following types of room heating are relatively safe for young children:
▶ Low surface temperature convector radiators
▶ Thermostatically controlled oil filled space heaters
▶ Fan heaters with the element inaccessible to a young child
▶ Air-conditioners
▶ Radiators mounted at least 2 metres above floor level

Specify radiators with rounded tops, not welded seams, to minimize the consequences of falling on them. Do not position radiators at the bottom of a flight of stairs.

Paraffin heaters must be tested for stability and must also have some method of securing them, to stop them falling over. They must cut out automatically within fifteen seconds if tipped over, and must neither have any unguarded flame, nor give off smoke nor produce excessive amounts of carbon monoxide.

It is important not to leave children
alone in the room even after a
good fireguard has been fitted.

Remember that any open fire or electric radiator may ignite clothing. Therefore:
▶ avoid long, loose-fitting or frilly nightwear
▶ avoid all readily flammable material in children's clothing
▶ use close-fitting nightwear made from flame-resistant material.
By law, all ready-made nightwear for children must be made from material which does not flare up or burn easily. It must comply with the requirements of BS 5722.

Floor coverings

All-over carpet is safest for children. It is softer and less slippery than polished floors. Avoid scatter rugs on polished floors.

Household furniture

Make sure that all furniture is stable and will not tip over easily. With young children, try to have rounded corners on tables and work surfaces. Glass-top coffee tables are best avoided if you have young children.

Check on the flammability of furnishings and fabrics. In general, wool is safer than cotton fabrics or synthetics. Many types of upholstery and padding are highly flammable and give off toxic smoke fumes. British Standard 5852 studied the effects on upholstered furniture of both a smouldering cigarette and a lighted match. Items which do not meet the criteria laid down under this standard have been banned from sale.

Furniture must now, by law, bear both permanent and display labels to indicate the tests to which it has been submitted. Green rectangular labels indicate that the match equivalent test has been passed. Red triangular labels warn that the item has failed the flammability test.

Nursery furniture, prams and pushchairs

Cots (BS 1753)

Cots must be of a solid construction with no projections or exposed sharp edges. The sides and ends must be high enough to stop an infant from climbing out. There must be no horizontal slats.

The minimum distance between the top of the mattress and the top of the cot should be 495 millimetres. The space between the slats should be between 25 and 60 millimetres to prevent a baby slipping through feet first. The dropside should have fastenings which engage automatically, and an infant should not be able to disengage them on his own.

The cot should contain no decorative transfers on the inside and should not include any materials which could be harmful to a baby. The cot should be labelled to show which size mattress is appropriate.

Carrycots (BS 3881)

These are usually collapsible and must be designed so that they cannot collapse after they have been assembled securely. Both the stand and the carrycot must be of a sturdy construction. When assembled, the base of the cot must be no more than 432 millimetres above the floor.

The cot must be made of safe, non-toxic materials, and the handles should be positioned so that two people can carry it safely. The cot should be provided with harness attachments.

Cot and pram mattresses and pillows (BS 1877)

Mattresses should be labelled to show the size of cot for which they are intended. It is very important to match up cot and mattress to ensure that there is not a dangerous gap between the side of the mattress and the edge of the cot.

Mattress covers should be an exact fit and should be made of permeable material or have ventilators fitted. The filling should be clean and harmless. Either a spring interior or firm polyurethane foam may be used. Handles should not be fitted.

Pillows should not be used for infants under twelve months and should carry a warning label. The pillow and pillow cover should be porous so that air can pass through freely. They should both be washable. Any plastic packaging should be removed and disposed of before use.

Baby walkers (BS 4648)

There is no good evidence that a baby walker will help an infant to walk any earlier and they are the cause of a large number of accidents every year. However, the reality is that many parents will want to use them.

▶ Remember that baby walkers are not toys!

▶ Take particular care that stairs, fires and doorways are guarded.
▶ Never leave your baby alone in a walker, even for a moment.

Baby walkers should be of sturdy construction with castors at least 50 millimetres apart. They should move freely, but should not overturn easily. The seat should be strong and made of washable material. The frame should be metal, with no sharp edges or open-ended tubes to catch baby's fingers.

Prams (BS 4139) and pushchairs (BS 4792)

Prams and pushchairs should be of sturdy construction and sufficiently stable not to tip over with normal use. The demand for inexpensive, lightweight pushchairs means they may not be as robust as the one you rode in as a child! Remember that pushchairs and prams are not designed to carry additional children or heavy shopping. It is unwise to hang shopping bags on the handles.

All prams and pushchairs must be fitted with reliable brakes which will operate on a slope. The brake must be out of the child's reach. As a safety measure it is desirable to have two separate locking devices.

Safety harnesses (BS 6684)

A safety harness should be fitted to restrain small children in prams, pushchairs, carrycots and high chairs. It should not be used to restrain a child in a cot or bed or in a motor vehicle, except in a carrycot which is suitably restrained. It is also advisable for a young child to wear a harness with a walking rein when out shopping with you.

Safety barriers (BS 4125)

Select a safety barrier marked with the British Standard number. They can be set up at the top and bottom of stairways or in a doorway. They are intended for children up to two years of age.

When properly set up according to the instructions supplied, a young child will not be able to jerk it free or unfasten it.

Playpens (BS 4863)

Playpens are designed to be safe for children up to about two years of age. They should be not less than 600 millimetres high and should have a detachable base, covering the floor area. The vertical bars should be set 75–100 millimetres apart. The playpen should have no horizontal bars on which a child could climb. When assembled the playpen should remain firmly on the floor and it should not be possible for a young child to open the fastenings.

When purchasing any of the above equipment for your child, look for the British Standards Institution number.

NOTE. This information is contained in the BSI booklet 'Playing Safe With British Standards'. For more information about British Standards contact the BSI public relations department, 2 Park Street, London W1A 2BS.

Designing for fire safety

Most fatal burning accidents relate to house fires. Death is due to the inhalation of smoke and toxic fumes rather than to burns.

Most house fires that result in fatalities occur when the family is asleep. An inexpensive, properly installed smoke detector would save many of these lives.

Design or refurbish your home to minimize the risk of death from fire:
▶ Every room in the house should have at least two escape routes. This is particularly important when one escape route would take you through the kitchen or the sitting room. These are the areas where a fire is most likely to start. Escape routes may have to

include windows. If so make sure they can readily be opened wide enough by an adult to provide a safe exit.

▶ Group bedrooms together if possible so that, in the case of a fire, parents can account for the children and assist them to escape.

▶ Obtain advice on the installation and maintenance of smoke detectors.

▶ Adequate built-in heating is an important safety feature. All heating systems should be installed by a professional.

▶ Have electrical wiring and power outlets properly installed.

▶ Ensure that the kitchen stove is sited away from windows and that cupboards and fittings are not sited over it.

▶ Switches for the hob should be located beside it rather than behind. The area behind the hob should be fireproof. Stoves and hobs should be sited away from circulation routes.

▶ Store matches away from young children.

▶ Make sure cigarettes are properly extinguished and do not smoke in bed.

▶ Store flammable liquids safely in a locked cupboard outside the house, if possible.

What to do in an emergency

Most kitchen fires are the result of carelessness, especially when frying. If the frying pan catches fire do not try to carry it out of the house. Do not pour water on it. Turn off the stove, if possible, and put a blanket, damp cloth or lid over the pan.

Small fires can usually be dealt with effectively by smothering them with a blanket or rug. The use of fire extinguishers by untrained people is not recommended.

If clothing catches fire, put the child on the floor immediately to stop the flames reaching the face. Cover the child with a rug or blanket to smother the flames and roll the child on the floor.

If the house is on fire, get everybody out of the house at once by the safest available route. Do not waste valuable time trying to put the fire out. Inhalation of smoke and toxic fumes can kill very quickly. If you have to pass through a smoke filled room, drop and crawl to safety. Shut doors and windows if you have time and if you can do so safely.

Poisons in your home

About thirty children die each year as a result of poisoning. Approximately 12,000 children are admitted to hospital, the great majority being under five years of age.

Following the introduction of child-resistant containers, the reduction in pack size and strip packaging, there has been a marked fall in admissions for poisoning from aspirin and paracetamol. The incidence fell from around 7000 per year before 1975 to under 2000 by 1978.

The following types of products are the ones most commonly involved in child poisoning.
▶ *Medicines* are responsible for about 80 per cent of deaths and 60 per cent of admissions to hospital.
▶ *Household products* cause about 20 per cent of fatalities and around 25 per cent of hospital admissions. The most common offenders are turpentine, bleach, paraffin, disinfectant, perfume, alcohol and nail varnish remover. These cause 40 per cent of household poisonings. Caustics are less commonly ingested but have more serious consequences. They include caustic soda, paint remover and soldering flux.
▶ *Plants and berries* rarely cause serious trouble. The most common plant ingested is laburnum, which causes mild gastric upset. See also the section on poisonous trees, plants and fungi on page 60.

Poisoning

Richard's mother was distraught when she brought him to the Accident & Emergency Department. The two-year-old had vomited some brownish-black material not long before and now looked drowsy, pale and extremely unwell.

The house doctor examined him thoroughly and recognized that he was seriously ill, but was mystified as to the possible cause. He called the senior registrar, who came at once and assessed the situation. He noticed that Richard's mother was pregnant. 'Are you taking iron tablets?' the doctor asked. 'Yes,' Richard's mother replied, puzzled.

'Do you keep tablets where Richard can get at them?' The boy's mother hesitated for a moment before admitting, 'Well, yes, I keep them on the kitchen table so that I don't forget to take them. My obstetrician is very strict about keeping up my supply of iron. But Richard can't open the container!'

General resuscitation was commenced and an abdominal X-ray showed several rounded shadows in the bowel which were probably iron tablets.

Richard became even more unwell and was transferred to a paediatric intensive care unit where at first there was concern as to whether he was going to survive. The diagnosis of iron poisoning was confirmed.

Everyone was delighted when, after twenty-four hours of intensive treatment, Richard improved quickly and went on to make a rapid and complete recovery.

Richard's father later found the empty tablet container hidden under a bed. Distressed, his wife admitted that she did not always replace the lid properly because it was difficult for her to remove it each morning when she was required to take a tablet. But she vowed never to be so careless again!

Medicines that are safe in usual doses can be dangerous to small children, even in relatively small quantities. Iron and quinine tablets cause a disproportionate number of poisonings in children, but you should consider *all* medicines as potentially dangerous to young children. When medicines are supplied in containers .with child-resistant lids, always replace the lids properly after use. Keep all medicines, and other potentially dangerous household products well out of the reach of children, preferably in a cupboard with a child-resistant lock.

Remember the following points:
▶ Children under five like to explore and many can climb.
▶ Young children lack taste discrimination, and may swallow substances that an adult or older child would immediately spit out.
▶ Parents, and particularly grandparents, are often taking medication and tend to be careless where they leave it.
▶ There may be a lack of secure storage for medicines and household products.
▶ Poisonous substances are sometimes stored in former food and drink containers.

Prevention

The most effective way of reducing the number of child poisonings is the use of child-resistant closures and strip packaging for medicines and household products that have been identified as being particularly harmful or regularly involved in accidental poisoning. The British Pharmaceutical industry has adopted a code of good practice and now dispenses such drugs in child-resistant packaging.

Note the use of the words *child-resistant*. Such packaging cannot be made *childproof*. It serves to delay access to the substance in question and this is usually sufficient.
▶ Fit a special cupboard with a child-resistant catch in the bathroom and kitchen.
▶ Store medicines and dangerous household products out of the reach of children.
▶ Always use medicines and household products according to instructions. Read warning labels and take them seriously.
▶ Take your own pills and medicines away from the view of young children.
▶ Dispose of unwanted medicines safely.
▶ When visiting grandparents, look carefully for medicines or dangerous household products within reach of a toddler.

▶ Make sure each area of your house is 'poison safe' by using the following checklist.

Checklist for poisons in the home

The kitchen

		Yes?
1	Any medicines on the table, benches or windowsills?	❏
2	Any household products with 'warning labels' under the sink (except those in child-resistant containers)?	❏
3	Any drain cleaners, polishes or dishwasher powders 'within reach' (that is less than 1.75 metres from the floor)?	❏
4	Any foods and household products kept together?	❏
5	Any cigarettes or alcoholic drinks 'within reach'?	❏

The bathroom

6	Any medicines 'within reach'?	❏
7	Any old medicines, unlikely to be used again?	❏
8	Any cleaning agents or cosmetics 'within reach'?	❏

The bedroom

9	Any medicines 'within reach'?	❏
10	Any perfumes, nail-polish removers or other potentially poisonous substances 'within reach'?	❏
11	Any flaking paint which may contain lead (if in an old house)?	❏

SCORING (one point for each yes):

0–3	Much better than average.
4–6	Could do much better. (Do it now.)
7–9	Bad – urgent action needed.
10–11	What can we say?

Renovations and extensions

When renovating or extending your home, special care needs to be taken to safeguard your children.

The increasing availability of tools and materials previously available only to professionals has meant that renovations are increasingly being done by the 'handy' homeowner. While home renovations can give great satisfaction as well as saving on the costs, certain precautions need to be taken:

▶ *Removing paint*   If your house is more than fifty years old, paint removal by dry sanding, blowtorch, heatgun or scraping can lead to lead poisoning, especially in young children. The fine paint dust settles on the floor, especially in carpets, and can be extremely hard to remove. Toddlers then sit on the floor, play with objects in contact with the dust and put these, or their hands, to their mouths. Because of the dangers associated with paint removal in old houses, professional advice should always be sought.

▶ *Using power tools*   Children should be well supervised away from the work area when power tools are being used. Power tools also carry a higher risk of accidental electrocution than most other appliances. This risk can be lowered by the use of an earth-leakage circuit breaker. Power tools should never be used in the rain.

▶ *Using ladders*   Apart from the more obvious risks of falling from ladders, fingers have been lost when caught in the triangular braces used in most aluminium ladders.

▶ *Electrical work*   Changing light bulbs and replacing fuses are obviously within the scope of most people (always make sure the power is turned off first). However, do not carry out changes to household wiring. Apart from being illegal, you may put at risk the lives of your family. Always employ a licensed electrician.

▶ *Plumbing work*   Changing a tap washer can be done by many people. However, changing or extending any household plumbing should not be undertaken. Always employ a licensed plumber.

When carrying out renovations, always ensure that children are well supervised away from the work area. If older children want to help, explain the possible dangers and let them help, but keep a close eye on them. Helping with renovations can be a very useful learning experience for older children.

If your home is being extended by a builder and you must continue to occupy the home while the work is being done, keep the following precautions in mind:

▶ Do not trust the builder to keep the work area safe. Look out for water-filled holes, unstable piles of timber, bricks, broken glass, ladders and places where a child could fall from a considerable height.

▶ Younger children must be kept completely away from the work area. Use temporary barricades and, if necessary, replace them when moved aside by the builders.

▶ Older children will often show great interest in the work in progress and may wish to use the area for play when the builders are away. Use your discretion, common sense and maintain adequate supervision.

▶ Keep children at a safe distance while work is in progress, preferably where they can still see what is happening if interested.

Summary

By incorporating safe design features into your home, the risks facing your children can be lowered significantly. Special attention needs to be paid to the high risk areas – circulation spaces (particularly stairs), the kitchen and the bathroom. Also, always ensure that medicines and poisons are stored well out of the reach of children.

Remember that when doing 'handywork' around the home it is important to safeguard your children against the many potential hazards. For young children, in particular, it is best to keep them well away from the work area.

Chapter

4 SAFETY OUTSIDE THE HOME

The areas outside the home should provide an instructive, interesting, exciting and, above all, safe environment for your growing children. This chapter examines accident prevention in the garden, the garage and the toolshed. All these areas have potential hazards and, as with inside the home, careful attention to the design and maintenance of these areas will minimize the risk of accidents.

The garden

Special care needs to be taken in planning your garden to ensure that there are safe areas for playing. Activities associated with maintaining and enjoying your garden – for example, gardening, mowing the lawn, fertilizing and spraying, and having a barbecue – are all potentially dangerous, and safety precautions need to be adhered to so as not to endanger your children.

Planning and landscaping

To provide a safe outdoor area for young children to play in, the back garden should be within view of the kitchen and, if possible, the living room. It should be readily accessible from the house. If there are children below school age, the playing area should be enclosed by a fence at least 1.2 metres high, preferably with direct access from the house. Any gate in the fence should be self-closing.

Children should not have access to the roof, and ladders should be safely stored away. All paths should be at ground level and paved areas generally, including external steps, should be slip-resistant and designed to drain away surface water. Avoid single steps wherever possible and see that all steps are clearly marked and well lit. In general, avoid hard surfaces, as injuries on such surfaces will be more frequent and serious. Ornamental pools and fishponds should also be avoided, since even if they are shallow, a small child can easily drown.

Poisonous trees, plants and fungi

NOTE. For a comprehensive description of poisonous plants and fungi found in Great Britain readers are referred to the excellent illustrated guide by Marion Cooper and Anthony Johnson published by HMSO (1968). Reference has been made to this publication in preparing the following material.

Plants are not a frequent cause of serious poisoning in Great Britain. It is estimated that about 38,000 children attend Accident and Emergency Departments each year following ingestion of plants and berries, but in most cases, admission is not required and a serious or fatal outcome is extremely rare.

Most plants contain substances which in theory could prove injurious but many have either never been eaten or cause only trivial symptoms. For example, potato tubers are edible but all the green parts of the plant, including sprouting tubers, are toxic. Similarly, the fruit of the tomato is the only part of the plant that is not poisonous. There are also many poisonous toadstools and mushrooms in Great Britain.

Symptoms of plant poisoning

Nausea, vomiting and abdominal pain are the commonest symptoms. Some plants also cause diarrhoea and those with irritant sap can cause soreness or blistering of the lips and mouth. Some plants, such as cannabis and morning glory, and certain fungi, can produce changes in behaviour and mental state. Severe poisoning by certain toxic plants can result in convulsions and loss of consciousness and some, such as yew and foxglove, can cause heart failure.

Whenever plant poisoning is suspected, expert medical advice should be sought without delay. If possible a sample of the suspected plant should be taken with you for positive identification.

The following list includes plants and fungi of known toxicity that are found in Great Britain and have been implicated on a number of occasions in poisoning episodes.

Poisonous plants, shrubs and trees

Beech Trees   Beech nuts can cause poisoning. They cause soreness of the mouth and tongue, and larger quantities can cause more serious symptoms.

Castor Oil Plant   Chewing the seeds can be fatal. Necklaces made from the beans should be avoided as in addition to being poisonous they can cause skin irritation.

Daffodils, Jonquils and Narcissi   The bulbs have been mistaken for onions. When eaten they can cause vomiting, diarrhoea and abdominal pains. In more serious cases convulsions can occur. Recovery is usually complete in a few hours.

Deadly Nightshade   The berries are particularly poisonous. As few as five berries have been recorded as causing fatal poisoning in a young child.

Elder   Poisoning usually occurs from eating raw berries. They cause gastric upset. Medical advice should be sought if the symptoms are severe. Heating destroys most of the toxicity.

Foxglove   Of interest because it is the source of digitalis, used in the treatment of heart failure. The bitter taste of the leaves is a deterrent to children.

Elephant's Ear, Dieffenbachia   Popular house plants. Chewing the leaves produces redness and swelling of the mouth and tongue. The sap can produce persistent eye irritation. Keep out of the reach of children.

Hemlock   Used as a poison since Biblical times. Commonly found by the roadside in southern England.

Hogweed   Contact with the plant can cause stinging and skin irritation followed by blistering. Brown skin patches may persist for weeks.

Holly   It is not uncommon for children to eat holly berries, especially when they are brought indoors. It is not dangerous if only a few are eaten: it causes vomiting and diarrhoea but more serious symptoms are rare.

Horse Chestnut   Children sometimes eat conkers, despite their bitter taste. A mild gastric upset is all that usually results.

Ivy   Poisoning is usually due to the berries. They have an unpleasant bitter taste, so not many are usually eaten. Ivy also quite commonly causes skin rashes.

Laburnum   This is the shrub most frequently reported as causing poisoning in this country. Poisoning most frequently results when children chew the pods or the contained seeds. The flowers are also poisonous if chewed. Abdominal symptoms are followed by drowsiness and headache. If poisoning is suspected, medical attention should be sought promptly.

Latana   Young children are occasionally poisoned by eating the berries. Some fatalities have been recorded.

Lily of the Valley   A frequent cause of plant poisoning. Children are attracted by the red berries. Serious poisoning is rare.

Mistletoe   A problem at Christmas time. Keep out of the reach of small children, who sometimes eat the berries. Poisoning is rarely serious.

Monkshood   One of the most poisonous plants known. A number of fatal cases have been recorded. Best kept out of the garden if children are around.

Morning Glory   The seeds of some varieties have a similar effect to the hallucinogenic drug LSD.

Nettles   Commonly found in woods and hedges. The stinging hairs on the leaves and stems produce soreness, followed by raised white patches with considerable itching. Dock leaves, which usually grow in association with nettles, relieve the itching. Not poisonous when eaten.

Oak Trees   Children occasionally eat acorns, but they are not poisonous and there is no need to be concerned.

Oleander   An extremely poisonous shrub. Eating the leaves can be fatal. Abdominal pain, vomiting and diarrhoea are followed by visual disturbances, an irregular pulse and falling blood pressure. Urgent medical treatment is required. Best kept out of the garden if you have young children.

Privet   Eating a small number of privet berries can cause vomiting and diarrhoea, but serious poisoning is rare.

Rhubarb   The red stalks are edible, but many cases of poisoning have been recorded from eating the leaves. It is unwise to eat any part of the plant raw.

Potatoes   All parts of the plant above the ground are poisonous. More importantly, potatoes that have sprouted or become green are not safe to eat, even after peeling and cooking.

Yew   Fatal poisoning has been recorded after eating the fruit or leaves.

Mushrooms and toadstools

Considerable caution must be taken in picking and eating fungi. Identification is not easy. Contrary to popular belief, there are no special characteristics which distinguish toadstools from mushrooms or poisonous from non-poisonous varieties.

In a book of this nature it is not possible to go into further details about different varieties of fungi.

Children should be taught never to pick and eat any plants, particularly berries or fungi. Adults should not gather fungi for human consumption unless they can be positively identified.

Gardening and mowing the lawn

Young children love to 'help' parents in gardening. Older children sometimes enjoy a garden of their own. These activities can be fun and instructive as well as safe.

Sharp garden tools can be a hazard, though accidents involving

these are unusual. A parent and child being together should permit good supervision.

Mowing the lawn and the use of electric hedge trimmers is altogether a different matter. Children should be kept well away from power lawnmowers or rotary trimmers. This is because the rotary lawnmower (and other devices with a rotating action) fling stones or other objects like bullets, with great risk of eye or other damage even over considerable distances. Rotating metal blades can also cause terrible damage to hands and feet.

Older children and teenagers can sometimes be permitted to use lawnmowers, but teach them the safety rules:

▶ Always wear boots or strong shoes.
▶ Never allow hands or feet in the vicinity of the rotating blades.
▶ Always wear protective eye-wear (goggles or at least sunglasses).
▶ Never 'fool around' with a running mower.
▶ Learn to start the mower safely.
▶ Do not attempt repairs without being sure the mower cannot accidentally start up.
▶ Use an earth-leakage circuit breaker with an electric mower.

Always set a good example. Follow the rules yourself, not only for your own safety, but also as a way of educating your children.

Self-propelling and 'ride-on' mowers have special additional risks. They should be used only by the most responsible older children and adolescents and only after training and learning the manufacturer's instructions. 'Ride-on' mowers have the additional hazard of being unstable on steep slopes.

Fertilizing and spraying

Assume that *all* sprays are potentially dangerous and follow these precautions:

▶ Follow the instructions and warnings on the container.
▶ Do not leave either concentrated or diluted spray solutions in reach of children.
▶ Do not dilute or spray solutions in the presence of children. These are not suitable activities even for older children.
▶ Store garden chemicals in correctly labelled containers and out of reach of children.

Barbecues

Barbecues should be properly constructed, with a clear area around the barbecue. Barbecues are enjoyed universally, but can cause

Flame burns

Stephen was a twelve year old whose whole life revolved around music – he wanted to be a concert violinist. When I first saw him he had been admitted to hospital with horrific burns to sixty per cent of his body.

Stephen had recently done extremely well in a music exam and his family and friends had gathered together for a barbecue in celebration. As it had rained quite heavily the week before, the wood for the barbecue was rather damp and Stephen's father carefully added some methylated spirits to help the fire burn more strongly.

His wife called to him to collect the meat from the kitchen, and while he was away the fire began to die down. Concerned that it would go out, Stephen went to add some more methylated spirits – just as he had seen his father do. But he was clumsy and spilt some of the spirit on himself as he added it to the flames. With a rush the flames leapt up and Stephen's clothes caught alight.

Looking up at the boy's screams, one of his uncles grabbed a picnic rug and rolled Stephen in it on the ground to extinguish the flames.

The boy was rushed to hospital where prompt resuscitation saved his life. But the ongoing treatment spanned many painful months because Stephen had to undergo numerous operations to remove the dead skin from the surface of his body and replace it with skin grafts. Severe scarring and contractures demanded plastic surgery. But while movement was successfully restored to his arms, legs and neck, even skilled plastic surgery could not restore the full use of the boy's hands – he would never play the violin as brilliantly again.

Young children should be kept well away from open fires and open barred electric fires – protect them with a fire guard or grill. Children should wear tracksuit-style pyjamas and not flowing garments. Never use substances such as petrol or methylated spirits on fires. Teach older children to use matches safely and to light fires carefully.

serious burns in children. The following guidelines are recommended:

▶ The barbecue chef has enough to do. Designate someone else to supervise young children.

▶ If the wood will not burn, start again with fresh paper, kindling and dry wood. Use solid fuel firelighters if necessary.

▶ Never throw flammable liquids onto fires to make them burn. Deaths and terrible injuries have resulted from such action, especially where petrol and methylated spirits were used.

▶ Take care assembling and lighting gas barbecues. A spark or flame and escaped gas adds up to an explosion.

▶ Supervise older children so they learn the safe uses of fire. Show a good example as children (even young ones) learn from you.

Child drownings

There are between fifty and a hundred children drowned each year in England and Wales. For every drowning it is estimated there are two near-drownings requiring admission to hospital. Almost half of these are under five years of age and the remainder are equally divided between five- to nine-year-olds and children over nine years of age.

Sites where drownings occur

Rivers	23%
Sea	20%
Lakes & reservoirs	12%
Swimming pools	25%
Garden ponds	20%

There are three main factors involved in child drownings:

▶ Lack of adult supervision, especially in very young children

▶ Failure to separate the child from the water by child-resistant fencing

▶ A child's inability to recognize dangers associated with different types of water

Being able to swim will not necessarily prevent drowning. Knowledge of water safety is also important.

Prompt and appropriate resuscitation saves lives. If you have a swimming pool, all adults living in the house should be taught how to perform heart massage and mouth-to-mouth breathing.

Home swimming pools

Although relatively few homes in Great Britain have swimming pools, the dangers should never be underestimated. In warmer countries, like Australia, deaths from drowning in children under five years of age exceed deaths from motor accidents. Most of these deaths occur in home swimming pools, not in rivers, lakes, reservoirs or the sea, as is the case in Great Britain.

Aboveground pools and inground pools are equally dangerous. Even wading pools drown toddlers. Prevention of drowning requires constant parental vigilance aided by proper barriers.

Pool fences and gates should be at least 1.2 metres high with no horizontal footholds. Gates must be self-latching. The pool itself should be fenced off from the house and the backyard. Pool alarms and pool covers are never adequate substitutes for proper fencing and gates. Pool surrounds should be designed to prevent accidents.

Pool chemicals include concentrated acids (corrosives) and alkalis (caustics). Some give off chlorine gas which can be extremely

irritating as well as toxic. Pool chemicals should be kept out of reach of children and great care should be taken in their use.

Using the pool
▶ Discourage people of all ages from swimming alone.
▶ Ensure that all children, even older children, receive some supervision while in the pool area.
▶ Ensure that non-swimmers receive constant, close supervision. Never rely on flotation aids for poor swimmers or non-swimmers.
▶ Discourage children from diving from anything higher than the edge of the pool.
▶ Discourage underwater races especially underwater 'endurance' swimming. This activity, popular with some older children and adolescents, carries a risk of sudden unconsciousness and drowning. Teach teenagers the dangers of combining swimming with drinking alcohol.

Learning to swim
Attempting to teach young children to swim is no substitute for close supervision. Children are ready to learn to swim at around five years of age; few can learn at a younger age, some not until they are older. Involving very young children in water activities is mainly of value in teaching them to enjoy water.

The garage and the toolshed
Tragically, many children have died or suffered severe injuries from being run over while a parent backed the car out of the garage. A small child should not be able to reach the garage from the house unsupervised. What is more, neither the front door nor any other door opening to the exterior should open onto the driveway.

The storage and use of items in the garage and toolshed can also be a danger to children. Some garages house the family car and little more; others may contain a bewildering variety of tools, chemicals, and rubbish, some of which may be dangerous to children. To minimize the dangers, follow these precautions:
▶ Do not allow small children access to the garage or toolshed.
▶ Ensure that young children are supervised away from the work area for certain activities. It hardly needs to be stated that children and some spare-time adult activities do not mix. Examples are welding, glass-cutting, car maintenance and the use of power tools.

Checklist for safe storage of garage/toolshed items

Flammable Liquids

	Correctly stored?	Correctly labelled?
☐ Paraffin	☐	☐
☐ Petrol	☐	☐
☐ Turpentine	☐	☐
☐ Paint thinners	☐	☐
☐ Solvents	☐	☐
☐ Methylated spirits	☐	☐

Adhesives

	Correctly stored?	Correctly labelled?
☐ 'Superglue'	☐	☐
☐ Contact cement	☐	☐
☐ Other adhesives	☐	☐

Car-Care Products

	Correctly stored?	Correctly labelled?
☐ Brake fluid	☐	☐
☐ Polishes	☐	☐
☐ Aerosols	☐	☐
☐ Lubricants	☐	☐
☐ Detergents	☐	☐
☐ Antifreeze	☐	☐

Poisonous garden chemicals

	Correctly stored?	Correctly labelled?
☐ Insecticides	☐	☐
☐ Herbicides	☐	☐
☐ Rat and mouse killers	☐	☐

Other

	Correctly stored?	Correctly labelled?
☐ Drain cleaners (caustic)	☐	☐
☐ Paint strippers (caustic)	☐	☐
☐ Fibreglass products	☐	☐
☐ Paints	☐	☐

Handtools

	Correctly stored?
☐ Saws	☐
☐ Hammers	☐
☐ Planes	☐
☐ Axe	☐
☐ Knives	☐
☐ Chisels	☐
☐ Nails	☐
☐ Glass	☐
☐ Shears	☐

Electric Tools

	Correctly stored?
☐ Electric drill	
☐ Electric circular saw	☐
☐ Electric planer	☐
☐ Electric router	☐
☐ Electric sander	☐
☐ Electric jig-saw	☐
☐ Electric angle grinder	☐

Large tools

	Correctly stored?
☐ Metalworking lathe	☐
☐ Woodworking lathe	☐
☐ Wood planes	☐
☐ Lawnmower	☐
☐ Lawn edger	☐
☐ Hedge trimmer	☐

▶ Encourage the safe use of tools by children. Some older children will wish to use hand and power tools. Closely supervise these activities, at least until the child is competent, then watch from a greater distance.

▶ Always use an earth-leakage circuit breaker when you are using power tools or mowers.

▶ Teach older children about the risks from sparks, flames and fluids such as petrol, paraffin and methylated spirits.

▶ Children learn by example. Use tools safely yourself. Wear eye protection whenever recommended in the tool instructions.

▶ Ensure that all items in the garage and toolshed are stored safely. This means that potentially harmful items must be stored out of reach of children (that is, 1.75 metres above the ground and not accessible by climbing). All containers must also be secure and correctly labelled. Complete the following checklist to determine whether your garage or toolshed is safe.

Summary

This chapter has highlighted potential danger areas for your children outside the home – the garden, the garage or toolshed and perhaps a swimming pool or pond. Children should always be well supervised if playing or 'helping' outside.

Chapter

PLAY SAFETY

Children learn through their play. They explore and discover, learn how things work and learn about their own abilities. Children are all different: some are naturally cautious, while others are much more daring and likely to take risks. Play should be encouraged: it is an opportunity for children to learn the principles of safety as well as all the other benefits play brings. This chapter gives advice which will help you to make your child's play enjoyable, stimulating and safe.

Toys

When children play with toys they learn to manipulate objects, test things out, and discover how things work. While these are all important for the child's development, it is also important that toys are safe. The best toy for a child is one which is safe and suitable for the child's level of development and skill. Parents have to use their judgement when buying toys and to ask the question, 'Who am I really buying the toy for?' We all know that some parents buy toys which they think their child would like because it is a toy they themselves never had but always wanted as a child.

Accidents with toys occur for three main reasons:
- ▶ The toy is misused – for example, a child throws a wooden block at another child, causing an injury.
- ▶ The toy is unsuitable – for example, giving a four-year-old a skateboard or a six-year-old a chemistry set.

▶ The toy is dangerous. There are some toys which are poorly made or may contain toxic substances which could harm the child.

Selecting a toy

When choosing a toy, select one which is suitable for your child's age and interests, is sturdy and well made, and one which you think your child will enjoy rather than a toy which is the current fad. The ideal toy is one which can be used safely and which will meet the physical, social and learning needs of the child's particular stage of development. Do not buy the toy which you would like the child to have, rather buy something that the child will be able to understand, use and enjoy. These things are not necessarily the same. It also helps to remember that toys, especially those given to younger children, are not always used in the way intended. They may be pulled apart, bitten or sucked, thrown about, jumped on and have a variety of other rough treatments. For this reason it is important that the toy is one which cannot harm the child when it is used incorrectly.

When selecting a toy, keep these points in mind:
▶ Look for the CE mark. This is an assertion that the toy meets the European and British safety standards.

Lion mark   This indicates that the toy conforms to British Standard 5665. It is a mark of the safety and quality of the toy, and can only be used by members of the British Toy and Hobby Manufacturers Association.

BSI kitemark   This can be used on a product when it conforms to the appropriate British Standard for quality.

CE mark   All toys should now bear this mark either on the toy itself or its packaging. By using it, the manufacturer is claiming that the toy meets the safety standards of the European country where it is to be sold.

▶ Check for parts of the toy which can pull off to reveal sharp edges. If the wheels of toy cars pull off there is a potential danger. Wheels and tyres should be firmly attached. Small tyres can be easily swallowed or inhaled. Removal of a tyre might expose sharp axle rods.

▶ Plastic toys should be of firm, bendable plastic which will not shatter to cause sharp splinters when broken.

▶ Wooden toys should have smooth, firm edges and should not be likely to splinter when chewed.

▶ Painted toys should be made with non-toxic paints and should be labelled as such. If you are in doubt about the safety of the paint on a toy it is better not to buy it.

▶ Check for small buttons on toy animals and dolls which pull off easily and can be inhaled when these toys are used by young children.

▶ Ensure that the eyes in toy animals cannot be pulled off, and especially that they do not pull out to reveal sharp pins used to hold the eyes in place.

▶ Remember that most families have more than one child and that even though a toy may be safe for an older child, the young exploring toddler in the family will also get to play with that toy and may be injured by it.

▶ Stuffed toys should have seams which are securely closed and should be filled with clean, non-allergic fillings.

▶ Be careful with children's jewellery as it can be broken into small pieces which could be swallowed. Strings of beads should be strong and should be knotted between each bead to prevent all the beads coming off if the string breaks. Some jewellery is made from seeds. This should not be purchased, as occasionally plant products, particularly seeds, can be poisonous.

▶ Toys containing coloured liquids are potentially dangerous. Only buy toys with coloured liquids if the manufacturer states that the liquid is not harmful.

▶ If a toy has a self-retracting string, ensure that the string does not go back into the toy with so much force that the child's fingers could be tangled in the string. When the string is fully rewound there should still be at least 5 centimetres of the string left outside the toy. Make sure that strings attached to pull-along toys are not more than 60 centimetres long. Strings longer than this could wrap around a child's neck. In the case of cot toys, the string should not be longer than 30 centimetres.

Advice on some particular toys

The following toys are important and enjoyable for children. However, some advice about their construction and use is helpful.

Balloons

Balloons are better used for children aged five or more. Children have choked or suffocated when trying to swallow deflated balloons or when trying to suck them into their mouths to make bubbles. Eye injuries have been reported in children when balloons have burst directly in front of the face.

Chemistry sets

These should not be given to children under twelve years of age. They sometimes involve matches and flames and should be used with adult supervision.

Dolls

Eyes and buttons should be secure. Dolls which are taken to bed should be flexible. They are more fun to cuddle and do not form sharp or jagged edges when broken. If parts of the doll can be detached from the trunk, make sure that this does not expose sharp wires or hooks.

Electronic games

The main hazard here is the small battery, which can easily be swallowed and which may contain poisonous substances.

Kites

Kites can be great fun, but children should be told never to fly them near power lines. Make sure that the kites do not contain any wire or metal in their construction: only wood, plastic, paper, cloth and string are acceptable. If a kite becomes entangled in a power line it should be left there. Don't fly kites if there is lightning or if the string becomes wet.

Skateboards

Skateboards should not be ridden on roads. They are best kept for children nine years of age or more. Avoid steep hills and encourage your child to wear a helmet and knee and elbow guards.

Storage boxes

These help to keep things tidy but make sure when buying one that if there is a lid it is hinged, with a catch to hold the box open, so that it will not slam onto fingers. Warn your child not to climb into these boxes. If they contain a lock it is essential that the lock is one which can be opened by a child from the inside. Lids should be fitted with a rubber stopper which allows a gap of about 1 centimetre when the lid is fully closed. The box should contain ventilation holes.

Toys for babies

Remember that everything goes into baby's mouth. Toys for babies must be too large to swallow, too strong to be broken and have no points or sharp edges. Make sure that the narrowest dimension of any part of the toy which could be pulled apart is 5 centimetres. Pieces narrower than this can cause choking if swallowed.

Soft toys must be made of material that will not catch fire easily and will not pull off. They must be strongly made, so your baby cannot get at the stuffing. Cot toys should not have strings longer than 30 centimetres. As soon as your baby can crawl, remove any toys strung across the cot.

Toys which look like other things

Examples are erasers which look like pieces of fruit. Younger children may chew and swallow these. Magnets which go on to refrigerators and which are attached to shapes which look like food should be kept away from young children.

Trampolines

The main danger is falling off the trampoline or landing on the hard edge. Trampolines should be used with adult supervision and the area surrounding the trampoline should be grass, rather than concrete, and should be cleared of other toys and hard objects.

Tricycles

By the time children have learnt to go up stairs with one foot after the other they are probably old enough to ride a tricycle. Buy a tricycle without rear steps as this discourages carrying a passenger. A passenger on the back of a tricycle makes it much less stable. Warn your child about the dangers of riding downhill, as great speed can be attained and it is difficult to stop safely. Warn your child also of the dangers of putting fingers near rotating tricycle wheels. Check the tricycle regularly for loose, damaged or missing parts. Don't allow your child to ride the tricycle down steps or over curbs.

Water toys

Blow-up rings, armbands and other flotation devices are not life-preservers and should only be used under supervision.

Toys for different ages

The toys which follow are suggestions for children of different ages.

Up to one year
(These toys should be easy to clean, have no detachable parts and be well made.)

- rubber or washable squeaky toys
- sturdy rattles
- large, brightly coloured balls
- brightly coloured blocks
- floating bath toys
- strongly strung beads
- soft vinyl squeeze toys

One to two years

- large, smooth wooden blocks with rounded corners
- nests of hollow blocks
- pegboards with large pegs
- appropriately coloured and illustrated books
- soft balls
- soft, cuddly toys
- pull and push toys
- modelling clay
- toy musical instruments
- blackboard and chalk
- hammer and pegs
- picture puzzles (up to 10 pieces)

Two to three years
- miniature tea-sets
- miniature wheelbarrows
- appropriate books
- tricycles
- two-wheeled scooters

- wooden animals
- dolls
- dolls' houses and prams
- puppets
- boats

Four and five years
- magnets
- plasticine
- puzzles (up to 15 pieces)
- non-toxic paints and painting books
- skipping ropes
- simple musical instruments

- tricycles
- finger painting materials
- plastic scissors with rounded points
- simple construction sets
- clothes for dressing up
- farm sets
- toy telephones

Six to eight years
▶ construction sets
▶ kites
▶ musical instruments
▶ dolls, and dolls'
  furniture
▶ tool sets
▶ simple bat and ball
  games
▶ toy clocks

▶ sewing sets
▶ simple tapestry materials
▶ hand-held computer
  games
▶ water games (for use with
  adult supervision)
▶ cricket, softball and
  football equipment
▶ appropriate books

Over eight years
▶ equipment for hobbies,
  such as stamp
  collecting
▶ hand tools
▶ musical instruments
▶ netball
▶ microscope
▶ modelling and
  construction kits
▶ appropriate books

▶ puppets
▶ cash registers
▶ picture puzzles
▶ kites
▶ marbles
▶ skipping ropes
▶ hoops
▶ quiz games
▶ counting and spelling
  games

These toys are just a sample of the many available. An appropriate toy, if used properly and if made securely, can provide pleasure, learning and safety for the child.

Play in the garden

As children become older they spend much of their time playing in the family garden. As detailed in Chapter 4, it is important that the garden is securely fenced. In general it is better for children playing outdoors to be within eyesight of an adult and for the adult to check regularly on them. It is important to be aware of the tendency of young children to wander onto the street. Pay particular attention to the driveway as many accidents can occur there. A young child is not easily seen by a driver reversing.

Swings, slides and seesaws

Teach your child not to stand in front of or behind the swing. The swing should have a soft seat rather than a wooden or metal one and there should be a soft landing area. Swings should only be used under supervision. Buy good quality equipment. This is not necessarily the most expensive, but equipment which is sturdy and well made.

Check for cracks in slides and for sharp edges where fingers could be jammed or cut. With seesaws teach your child to keep fingers away from the fulcrum area of the seesaw where fingers can easily be jammed. Seesaws should have a block under the end of each seat so that hands or feet are not jammed between the end of the see-saw and the ground.

Paddling pools

Paddling pools and decorative ponds are places where children can be drowned. Paddling pools should only be used under supervision and emptied whenever they are not in use. Ornamental ponds should be covered with wire mesh. These can be a real hazard to toddlers.

Play away from the home

Outside the home warn your child to avoid dangerous areas such as:
▶ building sites, especially areas being excavated
▶ railway property
▶ rubbish tips
▶ drains
▶ underground holes or old excavation sites

These areas should have barriers to exclude children. Where there are no barriers, parents should exert pressure on their local council to have barriers erected. In any case, teach your children that although these areas look adventurous they can be very dangerous.

If your child is going to the local playground ensure that the playground equipment is safe. A survey of 250 playground injuries found that 30 per cent of all accidents resulted from injuries from swings and another 30 per cent were caused by falls from climbing frames or other structures built for climbing. Although adult supervision is important, this particular survey found that an adult was present in over 62 per cent of these cases but the accidents still occurred. Playground injuries occur more because of children's natural desire to test themselves and the playground equipment by experimenting in their play. Teaching children the dangers of pushing other children off playground equipment is important. Ensuring that the equipment is well-designed and that landing surfaces are soft will also help. As most playground equipment is provided by elected local councils, parents have a right to make their views known to the council if they believe that the equipment is not safe.

Swings

Injuries usually occur to young children who walk behind another child on a swing. Rubber seats on swings, rather than wooden ones, help reduce damage from this sort of accident. Check your local playground to see how the swing seats are constructed. If they are not safe, contact your local council pointing out this hazard. The more serious swing injuries occur when an older child jumps off or falls from a moving swing. Having a soft landing area underneath the swing helps reduce injury from this type of accident.

Roundabouts

The major hazard is falling or being pushed off in such a way that an arm or leg becomes trapped under the moving roundabout. The surface surrounding the roundabout should not be too hard and the design should be such that the space beneath the roundabout is covered.

Slides

Injuries usually result from falling off the ladder leading to the top of the slide rather than from falling off the slide itself. Again, landing surfaces should not be hard. Ladders with a tubular protective frame will prevent most falls. The ideal slide is one where the slide is made part of a grassy slope so that there is nowhere to fall to.

Climbing frames

Injuries on climbing frames usually occur when children fall or are pushed off by older children. The main danger from climbing frames is the surface onto which the child may fall. The ground surface should be of rubberised material or sand. Lower projecting bars on climbing frames can also be hazardous.

Guns and projectiles

Guns and other toys which fire objects have a fascination for children. Accidents can be prevented by not giving your child access to dangerous toys and certainly making sure that real guns are kept well away from children.

Gun play should be supervised. Guns should not be heavy so as to avoid injury when children imitate the frequently seen occurrence on television when one person hits another on the head with a gun. Be careful of guns which fire corks. Make sure that the cork is firmly attached to the gun by a strong string. Children should be taught never to point toy guns close to the face of other people. Guns which fire

Playground falls

Tim was very quiet and ashen-faced when his aunt brought him into hospital. His right arm was in a sling.

His aunt told me what had happened: she had been minding Tim for the day and had taken him down to the park to play. His mother had told her sister that Tim loved playing on the playground equipment and had been very keen to climb to the top of the climbing frame.

Tim happily ran off to the frame as soon as they arrived at the park. One minute he was on the second rung and the next a dog had begun to sniff at the lunch Tim's aunt had packed for herself and the boy. As she turned to shoo the dog away, Tim called proudly, 'Look at me, Aunty Anne! I'm standing!' His aunt turned to look at Tim who was standing on the top rung of the climbing frame. And the next second he had lost his footing and had crashed to the ground below.

Unfortunately, the playground was still undergoing renovations and the climbing frame was set in concrete. His aunt rushed over to the screaming boy whose right arm was hanging limply. She carried him to the car, carefully tied his arm in a sling from the car's first-aid kit, and drove him straight to the hospital.

After examining him, I sent the boy down to X-ray where it was confirmed that Tim had sustained a greenstick fracture to his radius bone. We set the break and encased his arm in plaster. By the time Tim left the hospital he was still very quiet but he was looking forward to showing his cast to his friends.

There was nothing that Tim's aunt could have done to stop him falling – except to keep him away from concrete-based climbing frames and not to let him climb too high. The main things to watch out for are that the landing surfaces are soft, that projecting bars are not hazardous and that the equipment is secure.

small darts and missiles are potentially dangerous. The tips of these missiles should have soft protective ends and should be firmly attached to the shaft so that they cannot be removed. Even so, they should never be fired at close range to another person.

Bows and arrows

These are fun but should be restricted to children over six years of age. They must have a protective, blunt tip which *must not* come off to reveal a sharp end. Children should only use the arrows supplied with bows and not fire other potentially dangerous objects such as pencils, sticks or wires.

Air guns

Air guns are not toys. The pellets from an air gun can penetrate bones, the chest or the abdomen. Children have died from air gun injury. One of the commonest injuries from air guns is to the eyes. In one-fifth of all eye injuries from air guns the eye is lost and in another two-fifths of cases some vision is lost. Air guns should be kept away from children under teenage years. If teenagers have them they must be taught to use them responsibly. It is illegal for children under fourteen to use a gun unless someone over twenty-one is supervising them.

Water guns

Be wary of toy water cannons which can have a range of up to ten metres and fire a very powerful stream of water. Water pistols, which only have a range of one or two metres are usually safe as long as they are filled only with water.

Real guns

Every year children are killed from the accidental discharge of a gun. Most of these gun accidents occur from guns kept in the parents' own home. The clear message is that having a gun in your home is a dangerous and potentially fatal situation for a child, so think carefully as to whether a gun is really necessary. The only effective way to stop gun accidents to children in homes is for the home not to have a gun. Gun accidents occur when guns are not stored properly, when they are stored loaded and when children have access to them. Guns should be locked away in a place where the child has no possible access to them and where the child has no possible access to the keys. They should always be unloaded before being locked away. Ammunition should be stored separately and also stored in a locked area. Guns should never be cleaned near children and when guns are being transported (for example, to the firing range) they should be transported unloaded. It is important to teach your child never to play with another child who has a gun.

Fireworks

All children love fireworks and bonfires. Parents must be aware of the dangers involved. Serious burns, especially to the eyes, are all too common. It is best for children to see fireworks at an organized display. In any case there must be adequate adult supervision – children and fireworks just do not mix on their own.

Pets

Pets can bring great joy to children. Children learn from pets about the importance of animals and the important part they can play in their lives. They also learn patience and tolerance.

There are two types of dangers associated with pets. The first, the one which everybody thinks of, is the danger to the child from a pet. However, young children, particularly those under four, can be dangerous to pets. They tend to be rough and tend to have difficulty understanding the need to be gentle. At a young age the child may be more of a hazard to the pet than the pet to the child.

Selecting a pet

When choosing a pet think of the maturity of the child, the maturity of the pet you are choosing and the animal's disposition. Make sure that the child is not allergic to the animal.

General advice when handling pets

Children need to be taught:

▶ not to disturb an animal in a sleep
▶ not to tease animals or overexcite them
▶ not to remove an animal's food
▶ not to put their face near a dog's mouth
▶ always to wash their hands after playing with a pet

Children also need to be taught some responsibility for caring for pets and for feeding them. The traditional pets such as dogs, cats and birds are often suitable for children. Some pets are much less suitable – for example, children have sustained severe bites from the sharp teeth of pet ferrets. It is best to choose a pet with which the child can play safely.

Animal bites

If your child is bitten by a dog or a cat, medical attention should be sought. The bite should be washed thoroughly and covered with a clean dressing. Even minor bites can sometimes become badly infected.

Advice for your child when a strange dog appears

Children should be taught to avoid strange dogs. Some good advice is that the child, if eating, should drop the food when approached by a strange animal. Children should be warned to keep away from animals who are fighting and not to attempt to separate them. If the child is approached by a ferocious dog the best advice is to stand still, keep the hands at the sides and not to look the animal in the eye. It is

better not to run. The dog will then usually lose interest and go away. However, this is easier said than done.

Diseases from animals

A number of diseases can be caught from domestic pets. These are usually parasite infections which are excreted in the animal's droppings and which can infect the child. Children can be infected from soil where the dog has left droppings, from contamination in children's sand pits if the animal has excreted in this area or occasionally from skin infections in animals. A good rule of hygiene is that adults as well as children should always wash their hands thoroughly after handling pets. Pets should be given appropriate immunisations and should not be allowed to excrete in areas where children play. This means that animal excreta should be removed as quickly as possible and children's sand pits should always be kept covered when not in use.

Puppies and kittens should be dewormed at regular intervals until they are six months old. Mother cats and dogs should also be dewormed while suckling their young. Your veterinary surgeon will be able to give advice about the best times and best medications for deworming. Listed below are some of the illnesses which can be contracted from animals.

▶ *Toxocariasis* This is a common condition where the eggs of the Toxocara parasite are passed in the droppings of cats and dogs. Usually children between one and four years are affected. The Toxocara eggs go from contaminated soil into the child's mouth, either by the child eating dirt or from putting dirty hands, which may be contaminated by the tiny eggs, into the mouth. The disease is rarely fatal but occasionally causes loss of vision. A high proportion of young dogs are infected by Toxocariasis. The condition can be controlled by deworming dogs and cats from three weeks of age and repeating at two week intervals for three treatments and then after every six months. Dog and cat excreta should be disposed of regularly and children's sand pits must be covered when not in use. Hands should always be washed after handling soil and before eating.

▶ *Toxoplasmosis* This is transmitted by cat droppings. It is spread in a similar manner to Toxocariasis. Infections often cause no symptoms but occasionally there can be serious complications, including blindness.

▶ *Cat scratch fever* This can occur two to ten days after the child has been scratched or bitten by a cat. There is redness and swelling near the scratch or bite, fever and enlargement of the glands (for example, the glands in the armpit if the bite is on the arm, the glands in the groin if on the leg and the glands in the neck if the scratch or bite was on the face or head).

▶ *Gastroenteritis*   Children should not be allowed near animals which look sick or which have diarrhoea. The germs they carry in their bowels can also cause diarrhoea in humans. Gastroenteritis in animals can be prevented by cooking pet meat. It can be prevented from spreading by washing hands after handling pet meat and not letting children handle sick pets.

▶ *Psittacosis*   This is a virus which is spread by birds in the parrot family and occasionally by pigeons and poultry. The virus is inhaled from dust in the bird's cage and can cause pneumonia. The birds themselves do not usually show any signs of the disease. It can be prevented by regularly cleaning bird and poultry cages to get rid of droppings, avoiding inhaling the dust from cages and not letting pet birds touch a child's lips. Children should be told always to wash their hands after handling birds and particularly not to feed pet birds from their lips.

▶ *Ringworms*   Ringworm is a skin infection caused by a fungus. As ringworms from pets can be transferred to children, the pet's fur should be checked regularly. A ringworm on a dog looks like an area the size of a five pence piece where the hair has fallen out. In cats the coat may only appear ragged and rough. Children should not be allowed to handle pets with any kind of skin disease and the animals should be checked by a veterinary surgeon.

Summary

This chapter was aimed at helping to ensure that your child's play is both enjoyable and safe. It is important when selecting any item of play for your child – whether it be a toy or a swing in a playground or a pet – to consider the appropriateness of the item to the child's stage of development and to make sure that the item has been manufactured in such a way as to present no danger to your child.

With certain toys (for example, kites) safe rules of play must also be taught. This applies to pets too – a pet should not be teased and it is best to teach your children always to wash their hands after handling a pet or after playing in an area, such as a sand pit, which may contain cat or dog excreta.

Play should be fun and stimulating, and above all safe.

Chapter

NEIGHBOUR-HOOD SAFETY

As children become older they have more freedom and more opportunities to explore their neighbourhoods. They may walk unsupervised to school, play in the local park and visit friends' homes to play. Parents also start to have more breaks from their childrearing responsibilities and may take the opportunity to go out, leaving their children with a babysitter.

Safety in the street

Some of the most serious accidents which occur to children are as a result of being injured by cars. Streets are designed for cars; they are dangerous places to play.

Teach your child never to run out from between parked cars to get a ball which has gone onto the street. When a ball has to be recovered, look carefully both ways *first* before crossing. The street is not the place for skateboards or rollerskates.

Further information on safety in the street can be found in the chapter on Road Safety (See Chapter 7).

Travelling to and from school

Follow these guidelines:

▶ Teach your child the most direct route to and from school with the minimum of crossings. (Primary school children need to be accompanied by an adult.)

▶ Walk the route with your child several times, discussing the safest places to cross. Involve your child in these discussions and help him or her to make the decisions about the safety of the route chosen.

▶ Whenever possible use pedestrian crossings or traffic lights. Choose a route used by other children but teach your child the danger of skylarking with others.

▶ When schoolchildren have to wait for a bus, the waiting area should be as far back from the edge of the road as possible.

▶ Be careful when stepping out from behind a stationary bus to cross the road. Car-drivers are supposed to watch out for crossing pedestrians, but do not assume they will always do so. Look carefully before stepping out.

▶ When waiting at railway stations, wait well back from the edge of the platform. Railway platforms are not the place for boisterous games.

▶ When travelling to and from school, the general rules for avoiding strangers will apply. (See page 121). Following a route used by other children, and walking with another child is good advice. This is in addition to the advice which must be given to all children not to talk to or go with strangers, even if the stranger knows the child's name or claims to be acting on behalf of the child's parent.

Visiting grandparents, friends and neighbours

Although your own home may be safe, how can you be sure that the friend or relative's place to which you take your young child is also safe? Visiting can be a potentially hazardous time as few parents have the desire, or courage, to check out their friend's house room by room before visiting with a small child. It is also a time when you are likely to be engrossed in an interesting conversation with less time to supervise your toddler.

▶ Supervision of young children is essential. Keep your toddler in sight at all times.

▶ Beware of friends' and relatives' handbags. The handbags of older women, such as grandmothers, may contain heart tablets or tranquillizers which could be fatal if swallowed by a toddler. Even the handbags of expectant mothers can be dangerous if they contain iron tablets: these can cause serious poisoning even if only a few are swallowed.

▶ The best rule is not to let your child out of sight. It is safer not to let toddlers roam free in a garden unless it has been checked first. If toddlers are playing outside, even under your supervision, make sure that the garage and toolshed are locked.

Babysitters

The most important thing is to know your babysitter and to know that he or she is a reliable person. In most cases young teenagers or children under teenage years who do not have the backup of readily available parental support are too young to be entrusted with the care of younger children. It is important to know that your babysitter will keep calm in an emergency. If you have doubts about their competence, it is wiser to cancel the arrangement.

Babysitter checklist

1   Children's names:

....

....

....

2   Name, address and telephone number of place where
you can be reached:

....

....

....

3   Name and telephone number of reliable neighbour:

....

....

....

4   Name and telephone number of a reliable, nearby
relative:

....

....

....

5   Police station telephone number:

....

....

6   Fire station telephone number:

....

....

7   Family doctor's name and telephone number:

....

....

8   Name and telephone number of nearest hospital
Accident and Emergency Department:

....

....

....

It is useful to leave a checklist for the babysitter and to remember the following points:

▶ Give the babysitter very specific instructions about your home and your expectations.

▶ Always leave a telephone number where you can be reached.

▶ Also leave the telephone number of a neighbour or close relative who can be contacted in the event that you cannot be reached.

▶ Call once or twice during the evening to make sure that everything is well.

▶ Tell the babysitter what time you expect to return.

▶ Make sure that all windows and doors are locked before you leave.

▶ Give the babysitter any important information about your children's particular habits or needs.

▶ Tell the babysitter not to open the door to any strangers and always to identify anyone who calls.

▶ Remind the babysitter that music or television should not be too loud, so that the children can be heard.

▶ The babysitter should know that the children must *never* be left alone in the house, even if this is only for a moment.

▶ In the unlikely event that there is a fire, the most important thing to do is to remove the children from the house immediately. The fire brigade can then be notified from a neighbour's house.

▶ Your babysitter should know that if he or she has any concerns you can be contacted and will return immediately.

Summary

Since the level of supervision decreases as your child grows older, it is important that your child is safety-conscious when away from home. Teaching children the safest way to travel to and from school provides an opportunity to increase their understanding of neighbourhood and street safety.

This chapter also highlighted the precautions necessary when visiting friends' and relatives' homes and when leaving your child with a babysitter. If you are leaving your child with a babysitter, you must be confident that your babysitter is competent to care for your child and that adequate support is available in the case of an emergency.

Chapter

ROAD SAFETY

Each year about 800 children are killed as a result of accidents. Almost half of these fatalities occur on the road. The greatest number of these are pedestrians – about 230. About 50 are pedal cyclists and around 80 are passengers in cars. In addition over 7,000 children suffer serious injuries as a result of road accidents. If allowance is made for underreporting, particularly of bicycle accidents, the true figure is actually considerably higher.

Road accidents involving children fall into three main categories – pedestrian, bicycle and motor vehicle accidents.

Pedestrian safety

From the age of one year, when children become increasingly mobile, there is a steady increase in the number of child pedestrian accidents, reaching a peak at six to eight years. After this age the numbers slowly decline but teenagers are still very much at risk.

Not surprisingly, young children have the majority of their road accidents on residential streets close to their home. In older children, accidents are spread more evenly over the road network although almost half of them are on residential streets.

Children from a deprived socio-economic background are very much more liable to be injured on the roads. This is largely because they are much more likely to be playing on the street in the absence of safer play facilities, and because they are more likely to be crossing hazardous roads on the way to and from school.

The most serious injuries are to the head, chest and abdomen. Limb fractures are also common.

Main causative factors

In the environment

▶ Main roads without sufficient designated crossing places.
▶ The child's view is obstructed by parked cars or other obstacles. Remember that a young child cannot see or be seen over a vehicle at the kerb.
▶ A lack of proper play areas away from traffic.
▶ Poor urban planning. Scandinavia has shown that it is possible to achieve a marked reduction in child pedestrian accidents by creating a safe residential environment, reducing speed limits in residential areas and providing adequate safe play facilities.

In the child

▶ Playing in the street without adult supervision.
▶ Children may be hesitant, impulsive or unpredictable when crossing the road.
▶ Lack of training. We should start to teach children about pedestrian safety from the age of three to four years. However, remember that children under the age of eight years do not readily understand the concept of dangerous behaviour and therefore cannot be 'educated' to become safe road users. They have difficulty in judging the speed of approaching traffic.
▶ Children have a limited view of approaching traffic because of their small stature. They cannot see over the bonnet of a parked car.
▶ Children cannot localize the sound of approaching traffic as well as adults.

In drivers

▶ Driving too fast in residential areas.
▶ Failure to appreciate the unpredictable nature of a child's behaviour in traffic.
▶ Drinking and driving.

Prevention

Young children going to and from school should be accompanied. By seven or eight years your child can be allowed to walk to school provided that a safe walking route can be planned. It is preferable that the child should be with other children.

Teach your children by example. Use pedestrian crossings whenever you take them out. But impress upon them that although pedestrian crossings are recommended, they should not assume that cars will invariably stop. Wait until the approaching car slows down before stepping onto the road at the crossing. Cross the road at traffic lights, whenever available. Cross the road holding hands and make sure that children understand that they must only cross with an adult. Make sure that they also understand that because they are not very tall, drivers might find them hard to see.

Warn them about the danger of running out onto the road in front of a parked car. Impress upon them that they should never chase balls or other children onto the road, or play on the road.

Let your children help you draw up a set of road safety rules for all the family to follow. Encourage them to join a Traffic Club if there is one in your area. Suggest to your child's school that they include

traffic safety in their health education programme. Get a set of reins for your toddler and try to encourage him to wear them when you go shopping or are out walking in a busy street.

Community groups should encourage local authorities to provide suitable play areas so that children do not need to play on the streets. Representations should be made for speed limits to be lowered in urban residential areas.

The Green Cross Code

The Green Cross Code is a guide for all pedestrians. However, children need to be taught how to use it and should not be allowed out alone until they can understand and apply it.

1 First find a safe place to cross, then stop.
It is safer to cross at subways, footbridges, islands, Zebra and Pelican crossings, traffic lights or where there is a policeman, a 'lollipop' man or a traffic warden. If you can't find any good crossing places like these, choose a place where you can see clearly long the roads in all directions. Don't try to cross between parked cars. Move to a clear space and always give drivers a chance to see you clearly.

2 Stand on the pavement near the kerb.
Don't stand too near the edge of the pavement. Stop a little way back from the kerb – where you'll be away from traffic, but where you can still see if anything is coming. If there is no pavement, stand back from the edge of the road but where you can still see traffic coming.

3 Look all round for traffic and listen.
Traffic may be coming from all directions, so take care to look along every road. And listen, too, because you can sometimes hear traffic before you can see it.

4 If traffic is coming, let it pass. Look all around again.
If there's any traffic near, let it go past. Then look round again and listen to make sure no other traffic is coming.

5 When there is no traffic near, walk straight across the road.
When there is no traffic near it's safe to cross. If there is something in the distance do not cross unless you're *certain* there's plenty of time. Remember, even if traffic is a long way off, it may be coming very fast. When it's safe, walk straight across the road – don't run.

6 Keep looking and listening for traffic while you cross.
Once you're in the road, keep looking and listening in case you didn't
see some traffic – or in case other traffic suddenly appears.

NOTE. The Green Cross Code is reproduced with the kind permission of the
Controller of Her Majesty's Stationery Office.

Bicycle safety

Children are particularly vulnerable as cyclists. 75 per cent of bicycle-
related injuries are in the ten to fourteen age group, but 25 per cent
affect children who are only five to nine years of age. In fatal accidents
involving bicycles, death is due to head injury in 75 per cent of cases.
Cycle helmets save lives.

Cycling is an activity that demands practice to develop skills.
Children should not only be taught bicycle safety and bicycle maintenance, they need to be taught how to ride. Older children, especially
boys aged eight to ten years, may appear to have remarkable bike-
riding skills. However, children do not develop the mental ability to
judge 'closing speeds' of other vehicles before they are about twelve
years of age. They cannot be taught these skills at a younger age.
Therefore children under twelve years should do their cycling away
from motor traffic. Insist that your children use cycle tracks, when
available, and encourage your local authorities to build cycle tracks.

Most overtaking accidents occur at night. Therefore cyclists
should only ride at night if it is essential and only with approved bicycle
lighting. Children should not be allowed to ride at night at all.

The great majority of serious bicycle injuries involve a major head
injury. Many of these can be prevented by a properly fitted cycle
helmet. Children riding bicycles, especially on the road, should wear
helmets complying with the British Standard. Teach your children the
rules of the road, preferably by riding with them.

Make sure that the bicycle is the correct size for the child. Many
accidents are caused because the cycle is too big for the child. Check
bicycles regularly to ensure that they are kept in good condition. Make
sure that the brakes work properly, the handlebars are tight, the chain
correctly tensioned, that there are no loose parts, and that the bell and
reflectors are in place. Encourage your children to do their own
regular checks and make sure they are done properly.

Make use of RoSPA's National Cycling Proficiency Scheme.
Schools should be encouraged to make use of the *Cycleways* Road
Safety Education package.

Bicycle safety

Ten-year-old Peter was in a mess when the ambulance brought him to hospital. As well as suffering deep gashes and abrasions to his face and extremities, X-rays soon confirmed that he had suffered a fractured skull and a broken leg. Cars, children and bicycles do not mix at all.

I later learned from a nurse who had been on duty in Casualty when Peter was brought in, that the boy had been given a bicycle for his birthday. His father had explained that he had bought one that was rather on the big side because bicycles are expensive and he wanted this one to last.

After some initial tumbles, Peter learned to handle the bicycle, but he soon became bored riding it up and down the drive. He asked his parents if he could ride his bike to school, which was only a short distance away. 'Lots of other kids do,' he explained. His parents agreed, but asked him to wear a protective helmet. 'Don't worry,' Peter argued, 'I'll be OK without one. No-one else wears helmets, and anyway, I'd look silly.' His parents, although somewhat dubious, did not police their request.

A week later, however, Peter was knocked down when he rode too fast out of a side street. He braked hard, skidded on some gravel and was hit by a car coming around the bend. He was not wearing a helmet. A neighbour telephoned for an ambulance, which arrived very quickly, and then located Peter's parents who went straight to the hospital. Peter's injuries were such that he had to stay in hospital for several weeks.

It is important that your child's bicycle is the correct size, otherwise it is difficult to maintain complete control. Make sure your child can ride safely and cope with roads and traffic before you let him or her out alone. Teach your child road signs and traffic behaviour. If possible, they should complete a RoSPA Cycling Proficiency *Cycleways* course before going out by themselves.

If your child cycles on the road insist that in addition to a helmet, he or she wears conspicuous clothing, readily seen by an approaching driver. Finally, if you live in an urban area, consider whether it is really worth the risk allowing younger children to ride on busy streets.

Children in cars

Injuries occurring in cars, together with pedestrian injuries, are among the most severe of any that children can sustain. You have a special responsibility for the safety of children in your car. You should set a good example by wearing a safety belt at all times whether in the

front or back of the car, provided that rear seat belts are fitted. Many children still travel without using any form of restraint. It is now mandatory to restrain children travelling in the back seat where seat belts are fitted. Everyone travelling in the front seat of a car must wear a safety belt. This applies to adults and children.

Restraints for different ages

Weight	Age	Type of restraint
up to 10 kg	up to 8–9 months	rear facing infant carrier or restrained carrycot
9–18 kg	9 mths–4/5 years	child safety seat
18–36 kg	4/5 years–9 years	child harness or seat belt and booster cushion

All cars manufactured since 1981 must have fixing points for seat belts fitted in the front and back. Since 1986 they must have seat belts conforming to the British Standard fitted as well. If you have an older car and cannot afford to purchase seat belts, enquire at your local Department of Social Services. There are a number of loan schemes established to help with the supply of infant carriers.

Difficulties may arise when more than three children are riding in the back seat – when taking a group of children to school, for example. Under no circumstances should two children share the same seat belt, nor should children be permitted to ride unrestrained behind the back seat of an estate car or hatchback. In a collision they face a serious risk of being ejected via the glazed area in the rear door.

A mother should never carry her infant on her lap, even if enclosed in her own seatbelt. The forces experienced in a crash, even at relatively low speeds would make it impossible for her to hold on to her baby.

You have a special responsibility for the safety of children in your car. Do not drink and drive, especially when carrying children. It is most unwise to leave children alone in the car, even for a short period. Even a young child can release the brake with potentially disastrous consequences. In many cars, the cigarette lighter is not inactivated when the ignition is turned off. There may also be matches left in the glove box. The upholstery of most cars is inflammable and the results of a fire could be disastrous. In hot weather children, particularly young children, left in a closed car can rapidly lose fluid, become severely dehydrated and develop a high temperature. Death can occur from heatstroke in a closed car on a hot day.

Tips for trips

Take particular care when driving long distances – on a holiday, for example. Road accidents are more frequent during holidays – traffic is heavier and drivers become tired and impatient. Cars are often overloaded on holiday trips or may be pulling caravans or trailers. Children may become bored and can distract the driver.

Make frequent stops and give yourself plenty of time to reach your planned destination. Avoid high speeds, limit night driving and do not continue to drive when you are getting tired. Share the driving, if possible. Ensure your children are well occupied and amused during the trip.

Summary

Road accidents are the major cause of accidental death and serious injury to our children. Many of these deaths and injuries could be prevented.

Start to teach children pedestrian safety from the age of three or four. Teach them by example. Children under the age of eight years should be under supervision whenever they are near the road. Do all you can to see that your children do not need to play on the road.

Teach your children about road safety from an early age and always set them a good example to follow. Make sure that your children know and adhere to the road rules if they are cycling. Ensure that your children always wear cycle helmets, especially when cycling on the road. Bicycles must receive regular maintenance. Set a good example by observing speed limits and the rules of the road. Show consideration for other drivers, cyclists and pedestrians. Never drink and drive, especially with children in the car. Adults and children must always wear restraints, suitable for their age, when travelling in the car.

Chapter

8 HOLIDAY SAFETY

Some of the best times for children and their parents involve discovering outdoor activities. Swimming, canoeing, sailing, fishing, rambling, walking, cycling, skiing, skating, camping and picnics can be healthy, interesting and enjoyable.

Unfortunately, accidents occur more frequently during holidays, and all outdoor activities have their particular hazards.

Knowledge, planning and watchfulness will greatly reduce both the likelihood and seriousness of accidents.

The beach

Although the beach can be a very enjoyable place to spend the day with your family, precautions may be necessary to safeguard your children against the sand, the sun and the water.

The sand

When going to the beach, especially if it is a popular one or if it has rubbish on it, make sure your children wear sandals or flip flops. Broken glass, ring tops or other sharp edges can cause nasty cuts.

The sun

The following recommendations apply mainly outside Britain, although you must take care if the weather is really hot anywhere. An increasing number of people are going to places like Greece and Spain for their summer holidays. When going there, always make provision for strong sunshine.

▶ All the children should take hats and T-shirts and wear them when playing on the beach.

▶ Make sure beach umbrellas are available.

▶ Take something cool to drink.

▶ Take suntan lotion.

Do not stay too long at the beach early in your holiday and avoid peak sun periods (between 12 noon and 2 p.m.). Get your suntan gradually. Sunburn is painful, and in children potentially dangerous. Skin cancer is increasing in Britain and Europe. The idea that suntans are foolish, not fashionable, is gaining increasing acceptance.

The water

Constant attention and vigilance are essential to prevent drowning accidents. Take these precautions:

▶ Very young children can be frightened by open water. Choose a rock pool or sheltered water for them.

▶ Use patrolled beaches wherever possible and bathe between the flags.

▶ Teach older children how to escape from a strong out-flowing

Drowning

This is a story of great good fortune which could so easily have been a tragedy instead. A family of four including six-year-old Ben were enjoying a canal boat holiday in August. They had stopped for lunch, and stayed inside the boat because of light rain. The canal was busy, with other boats passing in both directions at frequent intervals.

Ben decided to go ashore, and when he returned he walked around the outside of the boat. But he slipped on the wet decking and fell into the water on the deep side of the boat, hitting his head on the gunwale on the way. Because of the noise of passing boats, his parents heard nothing.

In the water, Ben was dazed but not unconscious. He found that trying to treadwater, fully clothed, was very difficult and he panicked. The more he struggled the more he gulped water and drowning seemed inevitable.

None of the four people on a boat passing at the time saw Ben fall into the water. However, a young nurse on an approaching boat saw the event but could do nothing until her boat was close enough. Four miles per hour seemed painfully slow under the circumstances. When she dived into the water, Ben could no longer be seen. By now, Ben's father had heard the shouting from the other boat and jumped into the water as well but did not know where to look. Fortunately, Ben was located quickly and was dragged, looking dead, onto the boat deck where the nurse carried out expert resuscitation. After a while he started making gasping efforts at breathing and slowly began to recover. He did, however, suffer temporary damage to his lungs from inhaling the dirty water and required several days in hospital before making a full recovery.

Never leave young children unobserved near water, even if you think they are safe. Young children can drown in just a few centimetres of water. Infants can drown in the bath or in shallow ornamental pools. Do not take children boating unless they can swim. Insist that young children wear suitable life jackets.

current. When you find yourself being taken out by an undertow, do not try to swim against it. Swim *across* the current, that is, parallel to the shore, for 10 to 20 metres. Currents are narrow and you will soon find yourself in still water. Now slowly swim back to the shore. If you are becoming exhausted, raise one arm to attract attention.

▶ Encourage older children to take part in lifesaving instruction at school.

▶ Avoid surfing near board riders.

▶ Young children should wear armbands or floats but this is not a substitute for adult supervision.

▶ Do not allow poor swimmers to venture far on inflatable mats or other flotation aids. Stay near them.

▶ Always heed warning signs.

Streams, rivers, lakes and ponds

Special care is needed in streams, rivers, lakes and ponds:

▶ The water in rivers and lakes is often surprisingly cold.

▶ Rocks, weeds, deep holes and strong currents are common features of rivers – even strong swimmers drown.

▶ Riverbeds change. After floods, shallow beaches may disappear and underwater logs appear in unexpected places.

▶ Diving is especially hazardous. Teach older children to check thoroughly for depth and rocks before diving.

▶ Never swim in flooded streams or rivers.

Boating safety

Many boating rules are common to rowing boats, canoes, motor launches, sailing dinghies and larger sailing boats:

▶ Watch the weather. Get an up-to-date forecast before leaving and watch the sky for signs of unexpected storms.

▶ Make sure the boat, its rigging, steering and motor are in good condition and that you have ample fuel.

▶ Make sure you have enough life jackets and buoyancy vests. Poor swimmers should wear life jackets whenever they are on the boat. All on board should wear proper gear when sailing offshore, including a safety harness when on deck.

▶ Carry a fire extinguisher on any boat with a motor.

▶ Take extreme care with fuel, fuel spillages, gas cylinders, gas leaks and stoves whether run on gas or spirit. Explosions or fires on boats are extremely dangerous.

▶ With small boats, step into the centre of the boat and sit down quickly.

▶ Balance the load so the boat will be stable.

▶ Encourage children not to stand up or move around the boat and not to sit in dangerous positions (the bow, the gunwhale or the transom).

▶ Do not leave without telling someone where you are going and when you expect to return.

▶ Boating and alcohol are a recipe for disaster. Safe use of a boat is at least as demanding as driving a car.

Details of safe navigation, distress signals, speed limits, boater's licences, emergencies at sea, procedures for 'man overboard' and 'abandoning ship' are beyond the scope of this book. Useful publications are available. Experienced boating people will always share their knowledge.

For the safety of your children and yourselves, keep within your own abilities and that of your boat. And remember – your children learn from you. Show them safe practices.

Canoeing

Canoeing varies enormously in risk. It is one thing to play around in shallow, warm, still water on a fine day and another altogether for inexperienced canoeists to try to negotiate broken water with overhanging trees and sharp rocks – or to be caught on a lake in a storm possibly without the skills or equipment for survival.

The skills of more advanced canoeing are best taught by qualified instructors at school camps or canoe clubs. Here are a few general rules:

▶ Anyone who canoes should be able to swim well.

▶ Wear like jackets (or buoyancy vests for those who can swim well). These should be of the correct size with straps properly adjusted.

▶ If planning a trip in a river or lake, three boats is a safe 'minimum'.

▶ In cold conditions, adequate clothing is essential. Children are at greater risk from exposure (hypothermia) than adults.

▶ If your canoe capsizes in fast water, try to keep upstream of it.

Water skiing

Water skiing is increasingly popular. Unfortunately, serious injuries often occur to the skier, people on other boats, swimmers and even people on river banks.

Learn the skills and safety rules from the experienced, preferably via a club. The following are important:

▶ Skiers should wear proper gear – life jackets or buoyancy vests and wetsuits or other protective clothing to prevent water under pressure entering the bowel or vagina (this is dangerous).

▶ Skiers should be good swimmers, know how to fall, and know never to place tow ropes around their neck, arms or body.

▶ Drivers must keep well clear of other people, all hazards and keep their boat and towing gear in good condition.

▶ Every towing boat should carry a backwards-facing responsible person aged 16 or more whose only task is to be an observer, so the driver can be told at once of any problems.

Falling in the water

Teach older children the survival hints, for any occasion when they may fall off a wharf, sea wall, boat, etc.:

▶ Stay calm, float or tread water.

▶ Call out or raise one arm.

▶ In fast rivers, swim across the current. You will soon be in slower water.

Other water sports

Board riding, scuba diving, dinghy sailing and yachting all have their own special safety rules. These are beyond the scope of this book.

Note that scuba diving claims more lives than any other water sport. If an older child or adolescent is interested in scuba diving, joining a club is the *only* way to learn the safety rules and to minimize risks.

Picnics, camping, hiking and country walking

Children as young as three or four years can take part in these activities. To ensure that each activity is both safe and enjoyable, follow these guidelines:

▶ If hiking or climbing, keep the distances and walking speeds appropriate for the youngest person.

▶ Proper walking boots are essential.

▶ Always take protective clothing and extra food.

▶ Tell someone where you are going and when you expect to return.

▶ Use hats and suntan lotion, when hot.
▶ Take insect repellant with you, if appropriate.

Choose safe campsites:
▶ Avoid close proximity to water, motor traffic, cliffs, steep slopes and other obvious hazards.
▶ Avoid camping under large trees – some shed large branches without warning.
▶ Choose cleared areas with constructed fireplaces where possible.
▶ Look out for ants' nests.

Keep food and water safe:
▶ Close attention to water quality, food storage and preparation will greatly reduce the likelihood of any stomach upset.
▶ In lowland areas even clear common running water may be contaminated. As a general rule, boil water from streams or treat with water-purifying tablets before drinking it.

▶ Keep food covered, cook it well and keep flies and wasps away as much as possible.
▶ Discard food not eaten at once.
▶ Wash your hands before preparing or eating food and after using toilets.
▶ Take great care with toilet arrangements. Young children who may be independent at home may need help when out in the country.
▶ Take care with utensils and dispose of food containers in an appropriate way.
▶ Keep matches away from young children.
▶ Supervise young children carefully when near open fires.
▶ Where fireplaces are provided, use them.
▶ Use solid fuel firelighters, if necessary, but never put flammable fluids onto fires to make them burn. Petrol and methylated spirits are especially dangerous.
▶ Young children, a caravan or tent and matches are a lethal combination.
▶ Fires from gas and spirit stoves in caravans start easily and spread dramatically.
▶ Avoid cooking inside a tent if you possibly can.
▶ Keep tents and caravans well away from open fires.
▶ Keep a fire extinguisher in your caravan. Keep a bucket of water at your campsite.
▶ Avoid using candles inside tents or caravans.
▶ Children should wear shoes and close-fitting clothes when near open fires.

Electrical storms

If caught outside when there is lightning and thunder:
▶ Do not shelter under trees, near light poles or other high structures. Stay inside huts, other buildings or cars, if possible.
▶ If swimming, leave the water.
▶ If in open country, sit down and wait for the storm to pass.

Safety in the snow

More and more children each year experience skiing holidays and visits to the snow. Both cross-country and downhill skiing can be learned and enjoyed even by younger school-age children.

Each year, there are many serious skiing and tobogganing

accidents, mostly avoidable. The following information will help make visits to the snow not only safer but also more enjoyable for you and your children.

Clothing and gear

Follow these guidelines:

▶ Adequate clothing is vital for protection against snow, wind, rain and glare. This includes head covering, goggles, anoraks, overpants, gloves and sunglasses.

▶ Hire or borrow proper ski gear. Do not try to 'make do' with ordinary clothing.

▶ Make sure that skis, poles, bindings and boots are the right size, type and correctly adjusted. If in doubt, ask a ski patrol person or the expert at the ski shop.

On the slopes

Follow these guidelines:

▶ Skiing 'in control' and on slopes appropriate to the child's ability is fundamental to his or her safety. Therefore, always arrange lessons for the first few days of each holiday, at least until the child is competent.

▶ Check the child's clothing and gear each morning.

▶ Toboggans are fun, but tobogganing is more dangerous than skiing. Choose a safe area, protect younger children and supervise.

Bites and stings

The United Kingdom is fortunate in having few poisonous creatures. It is unusual even for frequent walkers to encounter a snake. The European viper (also known as the adder) is venomous, but much less so than snakes from many other countries.

Bee, wasp and ant stings are painful, but usually not dangerous. If these occur, scrape off the sting and apply ice if the sting is painful. If the swelling is severe or the sting occurs on the face, seek medical attention. Some children become allergic to bee or wasp stings and suffer increasingly severe allergic reactions. If your child is affected in this way, seek medical attention. Adrenalin can be life-saving for people who suffer severe allergic reactions. Children can carry an adrenalin aerosol and can be trained to use this for severe life-threatening allergic reactions.

Horse riding

Although only about five children are killed each year in Great Britain as a result of horse riding, two to three thousand are admitted to hospital. Girls aged ten to fourteen years are the most common victims, outnumbering boys by six to one. This is the only type of accident in which girls outnumber boys.

Almost half the injuries result from falls from horses – most commonly limb fractures and head injuries. Horse kicks cause one-third of the injuries – rib fractures and internal injuries. Crushing injuries can result from the horse falling on the rider. These are uncommon but more serious. Horses also occasionally bite children or tread on their feet. Always avoid walking behind a horse.

Most riding accidents occur when the rider is inexperienced or as a result of the animal being startled.

The majority of children who ride now wear secure, well-fitting riding hats – in marked contrast to those who ride bicycles! Make sure that the riding hats conform to the British Standards.

Summary

Outdoor activities can be very hazardous. Children need to be well supervised and precautions specific to the particular activity need to be taken. Adequate supervision and awareness of the dangers are the best form of accident prevention.

Outdoor activities should be stimulating and exciting. If you take the necessary precautions to safeguard your children, then time spent outdoors is likely to be enjoyed by everyone involved.

Chapter

9 INJURIES WHICH ARE NOT ACCIDENTAL

This may seem an unusual chapter for a book about children's accidents and their prevention. However, the facts are that quite a number of injuries which occur to children are not accidental. These are injuries which are caused by a person who looks after the children. Sometimes these injuries occur as a result of negligence, sometimes they are caused by parents losing control and injuring their child. Occasionally injuries to children are caused deliberately by the adults who care for them.

It is important for parents and those looking after children to be aware of the problem of non-accidental injury to children. This chapter looks at some of the stresses associated with bringing up young children and recognizes that occasionally they can lead to a child being injured. It also looks at ways of relieving these stresses. The physical abuse of children, the problem of child sexual abuse and the ways in which children can be taught to avoid situations that could lead to sexual molestation are discussed.

Imagine one of those typical days when everything seems to go wrong from the moment you wake. The children wake up miserable and crying; at breakfast time the toast burns and your four-year-old knocks over a glass of milk; your baby has a temperature, does not want to drink and seems generally miserable. Father is away for a few days, and so is unable to give support. Your nerves are on edge and you wonder how you will get through the day. Things go from bad to worse: it rains all day, the washing will not dry and the children are in and out of the house putting muddy footprints on the carpet. Then, just as you are preparing supper you notice that your two-year-old seems particularly quiet. You then find the would-be artist in the sitting room trying to do a Picasso reproduction on the wall. Something almost snaps inside you. You see red (and lots of other colours) and you feel like tearing the budding artist limb from limb. Somehow, something stops you from doing it. You scold your child, clean up and try to hold on to your sanity. This does not always happen.

In some families, when the stresses of child-rearing are very great and when the parent has very little in the way of support, stressful moments like this may lead to the parent lashing out and injuring the child, sometimes quite seriously.

Of course it is not like this in all families. For some parents the whole business of bringing up children seems very easy – they seem to be naturals at it. However, there are not many parents like this. Some children are easy to look after; they are placid, obedient and never seem to get into much strife. Other children seem difficult right from the day they are born. They are irritable, very active (seeming to need less sleep than their parents), always getting into mischief and having the happy knack of putting on their worst performance when their parent is at their lowest ebb. For some parents, parenting does not come easily – they have difficulty coping with children, become upset easily and don't seem to have the calm confidence and tolerance that other parents have. For the parent who is not a 'natural', and who has a difficult child, the combination is a stressful one and certainly does not make child-rearing easy.

Somehow, most parents seem to survive the stresses of child-rearing but a proportion (usually unintentionally) do cause injuries to their children in moments of stress.

One particular injury can occur as a result of shaking the child. Occasionally babies who scream constantly are given 'a good shaking' by their parents. This can be very dangerous. Because young babies have very little head control, when they are strongly shaken their head moves backwards and forwards very quickly, and their delicate brain bounces inside the skull, sustaining severe bruising to the brain and sometimes breaking some of the small blood vessels which run over the top of the brain. These injuries can be very serious and lead to death or permanent handicap. If this chapter was to stress one thing above all others, it would be to warn parents of the dangers of violent shaking of young infants.

What to do when the stress builds up

When parents feel at the end of their tether with their children there are a number of things which can be done to try to cool down the situation. It is important to remember that it is not always essential to respond immediately to everything the child does wrong. In fact, many of the things children do are done to attract attention. A response can convince the child that he or she has now found a new mode of behaviour which gets extra attention. It may lead the child to do more of the same!

When you feel you are at your wits' end try some of the following:

▶ Ignore the behaviour. This is hard to do, but is effective.
▶ Leave the room if this is the only way you can ignore the behaviour.
▶ Ask your partner to take over for a while so that you can have a break.

▶ Count to ten before doing anything. This is an old remedy but it does help. Remember to count slowly!

▶ Try distracting the child and get him or her to do something else.

▶ Try to remember that there is more to discipline than smacking. This is only one form of discipline and in many cases it is not an effective form. Although discipline includes punishment it also includes teaching, showing by example and guiding.

▶ Pick up the telephone to call a friend.

▶ If necessary call a telephone counselling service – it is anonymous and can be very helpful.

Having coped with the immediate stressful situation, it may be worth having a look at how some of the stresses of child-rearing can be reduced on a regular basis. Suggestions include:

▶ Involving your partner in more of the child-rearing activities and making sure that you have regular periods of time which are your own.

▶ Use babysitters and go out occasionally.

▶ Enrol your child in a nursery school or playgroup. Very few people can be perfect parents twenty-four hours a day but if they have a six-hour break while their child is at a nursery, parenting is often much easier.

▶ Use some of the community health facilities available. For example, discuss the problem with your family doctor or your health visitor or seek help from your local child-health clinic.

▶ Talk to other people about child-rearing. You will be surprised to find that many others have these same stresses, and by discussing them with other parents as well as with professionals, some of the tension is relieved. You also pick up some useful tips about how others cope with problems in child-rearing.

Not many years ago people who felt they might be likely to injure their children, or parents who actually did injure their children, felt that they were unique. They felt that nobody else in the world could possibly have these feelings and felt very ashamed and reluctant to seek help. It is now accepted that child-rearing is not easy, particularly in our busy, stressful society. Help *is* available, and parents are certainly not criticized for seeking it.

Child physical abuse

Child physical abuse has been defined as 'a non-accidental physical injury to a child which occurs as a result of acts or omissions on the part of the child's parent or guardian'. Although this problem has occurred from time immemorial it has only been recognized since the 1960s. It is surprisingly common although the true incidence is not known, as many episodes are not recognized. A conservative estimate is that in a city of three or four million people there would be several thousand cases of child physical abuse each year. The injuries can be minor but can also be quite severe, including broken bones, burns or even death. Infact, child physical abuse is a significant cause of death in young children.

Who does it?

Most physical abuse is caused by the child's parents. This is because the parents are those who have most to do with the child and who are under the most stress in child-rearing. Parents need to be aware of some of the ways of relieving stress outlined above and also need to be aware of the dangers of smacking children.

The doctor's responsibility

When doctors see injuries in children which make them suspect that the injury might have been caused by the parent, they have a responsibility to inquire into this area as a possible cause of injury. This may involve asking questions about the accident and perhaps arranging a conference to discuss the case. The aim of this is not for the doctor to play at being a detective, but to find ways of looking at how the family manages some of the stresses of child-rearing and then to try to provide ways of helping the parents to cope with some of these stresses more effectively, so as to prevent injuries occurring again.

What you can do

If you feel that things are getting you down too much and that you are likely to injure your child, it is wise to seek help in some of the ways this chapter has suggested. Paediatricians and other staff specially trained in this area at hospital children's units and specialized staff at community health centres will be able to help you. They don't take a critical approach, are available to help (after all, that is their job) and can often provide considerable support and assistance.

If you have strong grounds for suspecting that a neighbour or relative's child is in danger of being abused, you could try to provide some help for the parent, such as by offering to babysit and by having the parent over for a cup of tea. Alternatively, you may feel it is more appropriate to inform the National Society for the Prevention of

Cruelty to Children (NSPCC), but it is important to feel reasonably confident of your facts before doing this. It may be appropriate to seek advice from the family GP, the health visitor or the local social services. In a real emergency, assistance could be sought from the police.

Sexual abuse

Sexual abuse of children has only been recognized in the last ten to fifteen years. It has been happening for much longer than this but until recently it was such a taboo subject that nobody would talk about it. It is an unpleasant area and life would be much less complicated if it did not exist. However, it occurs with surprising frequency although society is only now beginning to be able to talk freely about it. In the past doctors did not want to hear about it, other professionals did not believe that it existed and when parents knew that it was happening and caused by a family member, they felt there was nobody they could turn to who would believe them and take action.

It is difficult to know just how common sexual abuse of children is. What we do know is that it is probably at least as common as physical abuse. The evidence from several studies in England, the United States of America and Australia suggests that a conservative estimate would be that between one child in ten and one child in twenty has some sort of inappropriate sexual experience with an adult in their childhood.

Sexual abuse of children can be defined as 'the involvement of dependent, developmentally immature children in sexual activities that they do not fully comprehend, and which they therefore cannot give informed consent to'. Including 'informed consent' in the definition is important: young children occasionally do agree to some forms of sexual abuse or sexual exploitation but this is because they are bribed, threatened or coerced in some other way. They do not understand the significance of the behaviour in which they participate. This means that although they might consent, it is not really a consent which is based on a real understanding of what they are doing.

When people talk about sexual abuse they usually think of sexual abuse of girls. It is true that this is much more common, but it is important to remember that for every four sexually abused girls there is at least one sexually abused boy.

Who does it?

The adult readers of this book will be able to remember their parents warning them when they were children about the danger of going off with a stranger. Your parents did not say it was sexual abuse that they were worried about but this was certainly one of their concerns. The truth is that only one-quarter of cases of sexual abuse of children are caused by strangers. In three-quarters of cases the abuse is caused by a person whom the child knows and trusts, and in over half of these cases that person is a member of the child's own family. This is a fact which is very difficult to believe at first, but research in several countries has shown this to be so.

Clues to sexual abuse

The following things may make you suspect that a child is being sexually exploited:

▶ If a child talks about being interfered with sexually by an adult, this should be taken very seriously. Young children cannot make up these sorts of stories. A moment's thought will make it clear that young children just do not have the experiences which would allow them to give a story in explicit detail of some form of sexual activity with an adult. It is also important to remember that sexual abuse of children can occur from a very young age and although the problem peaks at around seven to eleven years, it can occur in much younger children including the pre-school age group.

▶ A child who mimics sexual activity regularly in play and drawings. This behaviour, although not proving sexual abuse, should make a person suspicious that the child is trying to work through some unusual sexual experience.

▶ A child who has precocious knowledge of adult sexual behaviour.

▶ A child with aches and pains and other symptoms always focused on the genital area.

▶ A child who has bruises, cuts or bleeding in the genital and anal area. Because these are unusual areas to be injured accidentally, some sort of sexual interference should be considered in these sorts of injuries.

What to do if you suspect sexual abuse

This is a very difficult area. When the question arises in your mind, part of you will want to block it out straight away, particularly if you suspect it could be caused by a member of your family. There are a number of things to do. One is to listen carefully to what the child says, reassuring the child that he or she will not be punished for telling the truth. It is very important to give your child this reassurance as many sexually abused children are told by the abuser that if they ever do tell anybody they will be punished or sent away to live in a children's home. It may be helpful to take the child to the children's department of a hospital where there are doctors, social workers and psychologists specially trained in this area and who have the skills of talking to young children and of carefully and gently examining them.

There are five basic rules to use when a child reports some form of sexual abuse. They apply to any form of sexual abuse including abuse from a stranger, acquaintance, a trusted friend, a family member or even the child's own parent:

▶ Tell the child that you believe him or her and that you are pleased you have been told.
▶ Tell the child that he or she has not done anything wrong.
▶ Tell the child that the adult should not have done this.
▶ Help the child to understand that you will do your best to see that they are not alone with that person again until the problem is solved.
▶ Seek professional help.

Teaching your children to avoid sexual abuse

Make your child feel confident. There is good evidence that children who feel secure and confident in themselves are less likely to be sexually abused than other children.

Children should know that when they tell you things they will be believed. If they grow up knowing this they will feel more confident about telling you about uncomfortable and potentially abusive situations.

Teach your children that they have a right to say who can touch them and who cannot as well as what sort of touching is acceptable. Teach them that it is alright for children to say 'no' to an adult about touching that makes them feel uncomfortable.

Children should know that if they tell someone that a stranger or relative has touched them in an unpleasant way, and they are not believed, they should keep telling an adult until somebody does believe them.

Strangers

Children also need to be taught about 'stranger danger'. For a child a stranger can be defined as anyone they do not know. Children are not able to distinguish potentially dangerous strangers from harmless

Stranger danger

Jane was cross with her brother, Tom. She always walked home from school with him and some of his friends, but today he was late because he wanted to play a quick game of football in the playground. He wouldn't let her go home alone and had made her sit waiting, banging her heels against the wall in the late afternoon sunshine.

When they did eventually start for home, she dawdled, deliberately lagging behind to show her indifference to him. She was a big girl now, and quite old enough to walk home by herself! Her brother and his friends reached the shop on the corner and went in.

Jane was walking slowly towards it, scuffing her shoes, when a voice called to her from a car parked by the curb. 'Hello, you're Jane Stevens, aren't you? Your mother told me that I could find you walking home. She thought you might like a lift.'

Jane took a step towards the car, peering in at the man. But her brother suddenly hurtled from the shop and seized her by the hand. 'What do you want?' he shouted at the stranger. Without a word the man started his car and drove away.

'Hasn't Mum always told you not to accept lifts from strangers?' Tom asked Jane, who was looking a little abashed. 'But he knew my name!' she exclaimed. 'Of course he did!' Tom answered crossly. 'It's written on the side of your schoolcase!'

Children should be taught never to accept presents or car rides from strangers, or to go off alone with anyone that they do not know – even if the person appears to know them.

ones. They certainly cannot tell by the look of the person or by whether they are being nice or not. Child-molesters can be very charming. There are a few rules which will help children avoid abuse by strangers. These are:

▶ Stay at least two arms' length away from any stranger.
▶ Do not talk to strangers even if they know your name.
▶ Do not take anything from a stranger even if it is something that belongs to you.
▶ Do not ever go with a stranger even if the stranger says that he or she was sent by a parent or a teacher to collect you.

Summary

The whole area of child abuse is a difficult one. It is highly charged emotionally and many parents find it difficult to discuss. The important points are:

▶ All parents feel violently angry with their children from time to time. Most parents do not injure their children but in some families loss of control can lead to the child being injured.
▶ If you feel stress and tension building up to what could be a dangerous level, seek help.
▶ Remember that sexual abuse of children occurs and that children who give a story of sexual interference, even if it is from a family member, should be taken seriously.
▶ Help your children to develop confidence and to know that they will be believed when they tell you something.
▶ Teach your child about avoiding strangers. A good technique is to play the 'what if' game – for example, 'what if a person you did not know offered to drive you home from school and said your mother had sent them to collect you – what would you do?' This sort of game helps the child to anticipate situations. It is a good method of teaching.
▶ Remember that raising children is fun but all families need help from time to time. It is much better to ask for help before stresses build up to the stage where you do something you have not intended.

Chapter

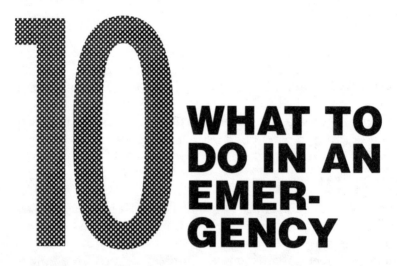

10

WHAT TO DO IN AN EMER-GENCY

Your child will be safer if you know what to do in an emergency. It is best to know in advance, as immediate action is often necessary. Note however, that this book is essentially about avoiding accidents – surely the best policy.

This chapter begins with the basic principles and actions of resuscitation and then details the steps which may be needed in the event of:

- cuts, grazes and bleeding
- nosebleeds
- burns and scalds
- broken bones
- spinal injuries
- accidental poisoning
- bites and stings
- choking
- strangulation

- unconsciousness
- head injuries
- convulsions
- breath-holding attacks
- drowning
- electric shock
- heat exhaustion
- hypothermia

Resuscitation

In life-threatening injury or illness, the airway, breathing and/or circulation are endangered. The ABC of resuscitation, refers to maintaining an open airway (A), sustaining breathing (B) and sustaining the circulation (C) of blood. The aim is to ensure a continuing supply of blood and oxygen to the brain, heart and other vital organs.

Regardless of the cause of the emergency, successfully maintaining the ABC gives time for whatever more specific treatment might be needed.

The airway, breathing and circulation may be threatened individually or together. For example, uncontrolled severe bleeding will endanger the circulation alone. If allowed to continue, the heart will not have enough blood to pump to the vital organs. More often, there is a sequence – anything which obstructs the airway will prevent normal breathing, leading to lack of oxygen in the blood and then to failure of circulation.

In an unconscious person, the muscle tone which keeps the throat open is lost and the tongue flops towards the back of the throat, thus obstructing the airway. This can be overcome by correct positioning of the head, neck and jaw.

Breathing will be affected by an inadequate airway, and also if the brain's control of breathing is affected as a result, for example, of injury or certain drugs. Effectively done mouth-to-mouth resuscitation can substitute, temporarily, for the child's own breathing.

Circulation will be affected by lack of oxygen and anything else which affects the heart's ability to pump or the blood vessels' ability to contain and direct the blood effectively. External cardiac compression is a means of temporarily sustaining some circulation until the heart's functioning is restored.

In an emergency, follow these steps:

▶ Protect the child from further injury (move him or her out of the water, away from smoke and fire, etc.).

▶ Control obvious severe bleeding.

▶ **A**   Maintain the Airway.

Place the child on his or her side, with the face positioned partly downwards to help drainage of fluid from the airway. Quickly clear the mouth of food and vomit.

Tilt the head back and chin up (this moves the tongue forwards and out of the airway). Listen and watch for breathing (sounds of air movement, chest movements).

▶ **B**   If no breathing, maintain Breathing by the mouth-to-mouth method:

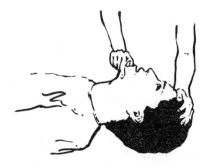

Turn the child onto his or her back and kneel to one side.

Tilt the head back with one hand on the forehead and top of the head, the other hand holding the jaw forward and slightly open.

Take a deep breath, open your mouth wide and place over the child's mouth. Often your cheek will prevent air escaping from the nostrils. If not, use the finger and thumb of one hand to pinch the nostrils together.

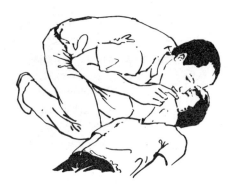

Blow into the mouth to inflate the lungs. The chest should rise noticeably then fall as you allow air to escape.

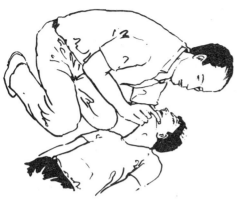

This should be repeated twenty times each minute.

The smaller the child the less force will be needed to expand the lungs.

If the chest does not move, check for leaks and obstructions.

Once the child starts breathing again, continue mouth-to-mouth resuscitation in time with the child's own efforts until his or her breathing is regular and strong.

Once breathing well again, place the child in the recovery position.

If no pulse is felt, commence external cardiac compression, checking often for spontaneous return of a pulse.

▶ **C**   Maintain the Circulation by external cardiac compression if you have previously learned this technique:

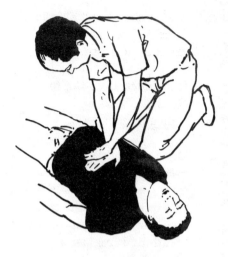

This is best done by a second person, the other continuing 'mouth-to-mouth' resuscitation.

Mouth-to-mouth resuscitation and external cardiac compression can be done by one person, but it is most unlikely that any untrained person could do these effectively in an emergency.

To do external cardiac compression, the child must be lying on his or her back on a firm or hard surface.

Place the heel of one hand on the lower half of the breastbone, place the heel of the other hand over the back of the first hand.

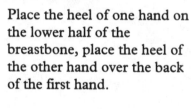

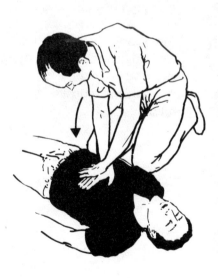

With the arm straight, rock forwards to compress the breastbone 3–5 centimetres, eighty to ninety times each minute.

After each four or five chest compressions, allow for one mouth-to-mouth breath.

With small children (six months to four years) use only one hand.

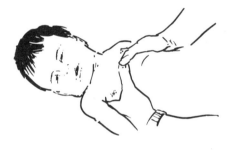

With babies, place hands around the chest and use thumbs to carry out cardiac compression.

A single operator must use a different sequence (for example, two mouth-to-mouth breaths, then fifteen chest compressions, repeated four times per minute).

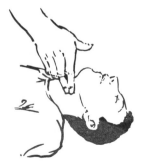

Check often for return of a pulse.

If possible, continue resuscitation until more expert help arrives.

Cuts, grazes and bleeding

All normal children suffer cuts and grazes. It is important to control severe bleeding, to prevent infection and, at times, to prevent scarring.

Control bleeding by raising the injured part, if possible, and apply firm pressure over the wound for five to twenty minutes (longer if necessary). Even severe bleeding from large arteries can be stopped with pressure. Apply the pressure with fingers or one or both hands, as necessary, using a clean handkerchief if possible as a pad.

Clean smaller cuts well (clean water, diluted antiseptic) and cover with a bandage (sterile or at least material which has been washed and dried).

With very large or messy cuts, clean obvious debris from the edges. Cleaning of the wound can be done better at the hospital or doctor's surgery. Gaping cuts may need stitches (sutures) or adhesive tapes to hold the edges together. Grazes (abrasions) often need only cleaning and application of an antiseptic solution. They usually require no bandaging. Deep or penetrating wounds and dirty wounds require medical attention. You need to ask:

▶ Could deeper structures or organs be involved? Could there be internal bleeding?

▶ Is the child up-to-date in immunisation or is additional protection required (for example, against tetanus)?

▶ Are special precautions needed against other infections or complications?

Nosebleeds

These can occur spontaneously in some children, usually older ones.

Have the child sit up, head slightly forwards and breathing through the mouth while you hold the soft part of the nose firmly between finger and thumb for ten minutes. After this, the nose should not be rubbed, picked or blown for a few hours.

Medical attention will be needed if nosebleeds persist or recur. Do not be alarmed by what seems a great deal of blood – a little blood goes a long way.

Burns and scalds

Follow these guidelines:

▶ Ice or cold running water gives excellent pain relief and reduces the severity of the burn.

▶ If possible, immerse the burnt area and continue this for sixty to ninety minutes. This must be done as soon as possible after the burn. The quicker an area is cooled the better the chance of reducing the severity of the burn.

▶ Do not pack a child's body in ice.

▶ Avoid handling, breathing on or coughing on burnt areas.

▶ Blistering indicates a deep burn which will require medical attention.

▶ Any burn which covers more than 10 per cent in area of the body can threaten the child's life. Hospital treatment is necessary as soon as possible.

▶ Children recovered from burning houses or cars may be unconscious due to lack of oxygen (smoke inhalation, inhalation of poisonous gases). Begin resuscitation at once (ABC) while someone else calls the ambulance.

Broken bones

Fractures (breaks or cracks in bones) cause pain, swelling, unwillingness or inability to move the affected part and sometimes deformity. Follow these guidelines:

▶ If necessary, remove the child from the source of danger. Otherwise, move him or her as little as possible.

▶ Support the broken limb and immobilize it to reduce pain.

▶ Give no food, drink or medicines. An anaesthetic may be necessary to set (reduce) the fracture.

▶ If broken ends of bones are protruding, cover with a clean cloth while further help is sought.

▶ In the case of an apparently severe fracture or dislocation, call an ambulance.

▶ In some cases, it will be possible for the limb to be supported and immobilized well enough for you to go to your doctor or hospital.

▶ Dislocations of joints are often as painful as fractures. Medical help should be sought.

Spinal injuries

Fortunately, these are uncommon in children. In younger children, most spinal injuries result from motor vehicle accidents. In older boys, diving and football accidents are more common causes. Very loose seat belts are associated at times with spinal injuries.

A spinal injury is suggested by lack of movement and sensation in the lower part of the body. If spinal injury is suspected, do not move the child more than absolutely necessary while awaiting the ambulance. If movement of the child cannot be avoided, use extreme care with two or more people supporting the child's head, neck and body.

Accidental poisoning

The aims here are to remove the poison from the stomach, skin, etc. before it can be absorbed and to support the child while any absorbed poison is removed from the body.

For swallowed poisons or unknown substances:

▶ If medicines, try to assess the number of tablets or volume of syrup then telephone your local hospital or doctor for further advice.

▶ If chemicals or household products, estimate the likely quantity, give milk or water (unless the child has taken acids, caustics, petrol or turpentine, or cannot swallow, or is unconscious), then take your child immediately to hospital or doctor for further advice. If possible, take with you the container or a sample of what you think has been swallowed.

▶ Do not use salt water to make the child vomit and do not induce vomiting unless advised by your doctor.

For inhaled poisons or suspected poisons:

▶ Remove the child from the gas or vapour responsible.

▶ If the child is not breathing, begin the ABC of resuscitation.

Some very powerful insecticides and other poisons can be absorbed across intact skin, in sufficient amounts to cause poisoning. If this happens:

▶ Wash the skin and contaminated clothing continuously for ten minutes.

▶ If any symptoms appear or if there is marked irritation of the skin, go to your local doctor or hospital.

Poisons splashed in the eye are treated in the same way.

Bites and stings

Animals bites and insect stings result in one to two thousand hospital admissions each year in England and Wales. Bites from adders, the only poisonous snake found in Great Britain, are extremely rare and are treated with antivenine, usually without serious consequences. Exotic snakes are occasionally kept as pets but rarely cause any problems.

Dog bites are the most common injury of any consequence. Dogs, and other small animals, produce puncture wounds and ragged lacerations which may require suturing. In toddlers the face is commonly injured but in older children the arms and legs are more commonly attacked. With some of the larger and more savage breeds, serious injury or even death can result.

Some insect stings, particularly wasp and bee stings, can result in allergic reactions, but most commonly produce only local pain (though this can be quite severe).

Emergency treatment

Dog bites   Superficial wounds from dogs and other domestic pets should be cleaned with an antiseptic solution. Rabies is extremely rare in the UK but in other countries, where rabies is known to occur, medical advice should be sought as a matter of urgency.

Children with severe injuries or facial wounds should receive prompt medical attention.

Insect bites and stings   Most stings can be soothed with an antihistamine cream. If there is a marked local reaction, with much local swelling or swelling of the face, tongue or neck, seek medical advice urgently.

An adrenalin spray can be provided for children known to be allergic to wasp or bee stings.

Snake bites   Seek medical advice urgently so as to minimize any possible reaction to venom, should the snake be poisonous.

In countries where venomous snakes are more common, the treatment advised is to immobilize the limb with a splint and elastic bandage until expert medical help is available. Failing that, a firm (not tight) tourniquet can be applied around the thigh or upper arm, depending on the site of the bite. Soft material such as a strip of cloth should be used, not rope or string.

Do not cut into or wash the bite or try to suck out the venom.

Choking

Choking is obstruction of the upper airway – pharynx (throat), larynx (voice box) or trachea (windpipe) – by food or some other solid object. It can occur at any age but is most common in very young children. The obstruction may be 'partial' (in which case the child can still breathe, with difficulty) or 'complete' (in which case breathing ceases).

Choking episodes are usually obvious. There is violent coughing, irregular noisy breathing, agitation and great distress, although with sudden 'complete' choking there may be no cough or noises of breathing.

In the event of choking, in almost all cases the child will be able to breathe after five to ten seconds. He or she can speak or cry but is coughing and breathing noisily. The airway may be partly blocked, or the obstructing object may have passed into airways lower down, or it may have been coughed out and swallowed. Go at once to your nearest hospital or doctor.

▶ Do not hold your child upside down.
▶ Do not give water or food.
▶ Do not slap the child on the back.
▶ Do not squeeze the chest or abdomen.
▶ Do not try to remove the object from the mouth unless you can see it.

If the child cannot breathe, speak or cry, clutches the throat, turns extremely pale or blue and/or becomes unconscious, the airway may be completely blocked. Immediately:

Put the child across your legs and give two sharp thumps with the heel of your hand, between the shoulderblades.

If the object is not dislodged, put your hands on each side of the chest and push inwards sharply, twice, a few seconds apart.

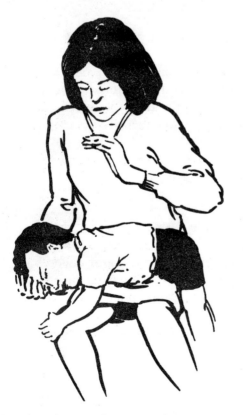 

If the child still cannot breathe, place him or her in front of you, facing away, and with your arms around the child and hands clasped firmly together under the ribs, pull back sharply in a backwards/upwards direction.

Attempt to remove the object with the finger over the back of the tongue and into the throat, sweeping from side to side.

If the obstruction has been dislodged, artificial breathing and cardiac compression may still be necessary. Follow the ABC of resuscitation.

Strangulation

Strangulation occurs when the airway and circulation are cut off by something caught tightly around the neck. Accidental strangulation can occasionally be caused in young children by curtain cords or even clothing, and in older children by their playing with ropes or clotheslines.

Do not delay! Remove the strangulating object and begin the ABC of resuscitation while an ambulance is called.

Unconsciousness

Whether or not the cause is apparent, unconsciousness in a child must always be taken seriously. If breathing is absent, commence the ABC of resuscitation immediately. If the child is breathing, proceed at once to the nearest hospital or doctor, observing the child carefully on the way in case ABC becomes necessary.

Head injuries

Head injuries can immediately threaten life if the airway, breathing or circulation are compromised. This may occur from direct brain injury, resultant bleeding or brain swelling, or severe blood loss.

In severe head injuries, there may be loss of reflexes protecting the airway along with much clotted blood threatening to obstruct the airway. Clearing the airway, then posturing the child and assisting breathing between the time of the injury and arrival at the hospital gives the child the best chance of survival with as little damage as possible.

Concussion refers to milder head injuries, where there may be brief loss of consciousness, vomiting, headache and drowsiness.

Any loss of consciousness following a head injury, either immediately or later, indicates the need for urgent medical assessment.

Convulsions

Convulsions are also known as fits, epileptic fits or seizures. There are many types of convulsions, some difficult to distinguish from breath-holding attacks or other events. Sudden loss of consciousness, rhythmic jerky movements of arms and/or legs, irregular breathing and then sleepiness is more typical of convulsions than of other episodes.

Seeing a child having a convulsion frightens most people. Most convulsions cease spontaneously and cause no harm, but they can be dangerous if they threaten the airway or breathing, or if they continue unabated over hours.

If your child has a convulsion:

▶ Move the child to a safer area, if necessary.
▶ Place him or her in the recovery position (page 125).
▶ Do not try to stop the abnormal movements or put anything in the child's mouth.
▶ Allow the child to sleep after the convulsion.
▶ If this is the first convulsion, or if the reason for the convulsion is not known, go to the nearest hospital or your doctor.
▶ If the convulsion does not stop after five to ten minutes, call your doctor or go to the nearest hospital.
▶ While the airway should be protected (page 123), it is unusual for mouth-to-mouth resuscitation to be required.

Breath-holding attacks

Breath-holding attacks occur in some young children, are frightening to parents and are often mistaken for convulsions. Breath-holding attacks

▶ almost always follow some upset, frustration or minor injury
▶ are always 'self-limiting'
▶ are associated with the child not breathing, going blue or pale and often losing consciousness briefly

No treatment is required apart from placing the child in the recovery position. Parents often cope better with breath-holding attacks if they know they can do mouth-to-mouth resuscitation, should it be necessary.

Drowning

If you are faced with rescuing a drowning child:

▶ Reach out to the child, if possible. Use anything to extend your reach (a branch, towel, belt, etc.).
▶ Throw anything which will float to the child (a beach ball, surf mat, etc.).
▶ Wade out if possible. In flowing water, use a 'human chain' if this is possible.
▶ Row or paddle to the child if any suitable craft is available.
▶ Tow the child only if you are a strong swimmer with training in lifesaving. Poor swimmers or inexperienced rescuers often drown themselves.
▶ Shout for extra help while removing the child from the water.
▶ Hold the child's head down for a few seconds to drain water from the airways.
▶ In some situations rescue assessment and resuscitation can begin while you are wading ashore with the child.
▶ If the child is unconscious, limp, blue or pale, and not breathing, begin mouth-to-mouth resuscitation at once.
▶ If a pulse cannot be felt, also begin external cardiac compression at once.
▶ Do not give up before the ambulance arrives.
▶ Children who quickly recover with resuscitation should nevertheless be taken to hospital, as lung problems can still occur in the next few hours.

Electric shock

Follow these guidelines:
- ▶ Shout for extra help.
- ▶ Always turn off the power before touching the child. If this is not possible, push the child away from the power source with a broom handle, wooden chair or another nonconducting object.
- ▶ If the child is unconscious, not breathing and pulseless, begin the ABC of resuscitation at once.
- ▶ Do not stop your efforts before the ambulance officers arrive.
- ▶ Even if the child seems to recover quickly, observation in hospital will be necessary.

Heat exhaustion

This is uncommon in children. Do not leave babies or young children locked in cars, even for short periods, and do not allow older children to run in long competitive events in very hot weather unless they have trained in similar conditions and over similar distances.

During unavoidable activity in very hot conditions, give fluids frequently. If heat exhaustion is suspected (muscle cramps, dizziness, nausea, headache, rapid pulse, cool face and limbs, abnormally low or high temperature), go immediately to your doctor or hospital.

Hypothermia

Hypothermia or 'exposure' is uncommon in children. However, it may occur to children during mishaps when mountain climbing, walking, boating or skiing. It is caused by body cooling (wind, water, cold conditions, inadequate clothing and shelter), and made worse by further activity and lack of food.

Indications of hypothermia include shivering, inappropriate speech and actions, unsteady walking, frequent falling and muscle cramps.

Hypothermia will develop more quickly in infants and children than in adults. Take action as soon as it is suspected.
- ▶ Find shelter.
- ▶ Change into dry clothes.
- ▶ Warm the child by wrapping him or her in blankets or by placing him or her against other people.
- ▶ Do not allow the child to do any activity.
- ▶ Do not apply anything hot.

▶ If possible, give warm fluids but no alcohol.

Summary

Knowing how to give first-aid treatment to your child in an emergency is very important. This chapter has explained resuscitation techniques as well as the recommended treatments for the many injuries that your child may receive at one time or another.

Of course, accident prevention is by far the best policy, but if an emergency does occur, knowing how to treat your child will help increase your peace of mind and may save your child's life.

DIRECTORY OF AGENCIES INVOLVED IN CHILD SAFETY

National agencies

Association for Consumer Research,
(Consumers Association)
2 Marylebone Road, London NW1 4DX
Tel: (071) 486 5544
Publication: *Which?* Magazine

British Association of Paediatric Surgeons
c/o Royal College of Surgeons of Edinburgh
Nicholson Street, Edinburgh EH8 9DW
Tel: (031) 332 2525

British Paediatric Association
5 St Andrews Place, Regents Park, London NW1 4LB
Tel: (071) 486 6151
The BPA has a Joint Standing Committee with the BAPS on
Childhood Accidents.

✳ **British Standards Institution**
Public Relations Department
2 Park Street, London W1A 2BS
Tel: (071) 629 9000
Produces British Standards for a wide range of nursery goods and
childrens equipment.

✳ **Child Accident Prevention Trust**
28 Portland Place, London W1N 4DE
Tel: (071) 636 2525
Concerned with all aspects of child safety education and research.

Consumer Safety Unit Department of Trade and Industry
10-18 Victoria Street London SW1H 0NN
Produces the Home Accident Surveillance System and the Home
and Leisure Accident Surveillance System.
HASS monitors home and (more recently) leisure accidents
presenting to Accident and Emergency Departments at a rolling
sample of twenty hospitals in England and Wales.

Health Visitors Association
36 Eccleston Square, London SW1
Tel: (071) 834 9523

National Children's Bureau
8 Wakley Street, London EC1
Tel: (071) 278 9441

National Society for the Prevention of Cruelty to Children
67 Saffron Hill, London EC1
Tel: (071) 242 1626

 National Playing Fields Association
25 Ovington Square, London SW3 1LQ
Tel: (071) 584 6445
Concerned with the preservation, improvement and safety of
playing fields, playgrounds and play spaces for children and the
handicapped.

Parliamentary Advisory Council on Transport Safety
c/o Dept of Civil Engineering, Imperial College, London SW7
2BU
Tel: (071) 589 5111
Provides MPs with information on road and traffic safety. Involved
with legislation to improve safety of children in cars.

Royal Society for the Prevention of Accidents
Cannon House, The Priory, Queensway, Birmingham
Tel: (021) 200 2461
Concerned with all aspects of safety in adults and children. Has
division responsible for Home Safety, Occupational Safety and
Safety Education.

Scottish Accident Prevention Council
Slateford House, Lanark Road, Edinburgh EH14 1TL
Tel: (031) 444 1155
Prevention of accidents in all age groups.

✳ The Royal Life Saving Society UK
Mountbatten House, Studley, Warwickshire B80 7NN
Tel: (052785) 3943
Concerned with all aspects of water safety.

Local agencies

Accident Prevention Advisory Services
Contact the Health Education Officer or Health Promotion Officer
at your Local District Health Authority.

Road Safety Services and Social Services
See under county, district or local council in the phone directory.

INDEX